heaven

RYLAND
PETERS
& SMALL

LONDON NEW YORK

First published in the
United Kingdom in 2008
by Ryland Peters & Small
20–21 Jockey's Fields
London WC1R 4BW
www.rylandpeters.com

10 9 8 7 6 5

Some of the recipes in this book have
been published previously by Ryland
Peters & Small in *Cupcakes*.

ISBN: 978-1-84597-684-2

A CIP record for this book is available
from the British Library.

Printed and bound in China.

Designer Carl Hodson
Editor Céline Hughes
Production Manager Patricia Harrington
Art Director Leslie Harrington
Publishing Director Alison Starling

Food stylist Linda Tubby
Prop stylist Helen Trent
Indexer Hilary Bird

The publisher would like to thank
the Cakes Cookies & Crafts Shop for
their kind donation of cupcake cases.
Visit their website at:
www.cakescookiesandcraftsshop.co.uk

CUPCAKE heaven

Susannah Blake

photography by Martin Brigdale

CUPCAKE

introduction

Who knows why cupcakes are so irresistible? Is it their individual size? Is it their delightful frostings and decorations? Is it their pretty paper cases? Or is it just that they're so damn cute? A whole, wickedly indulgent cake in miniature – all to yourself! Whatever the answer, the truth is undeniable – no one is able to resist their oh-so-sweet charms!

Cupcake time

The fabulous thing about cupcakes is that they really do suit any occasion – whether it's a sugary treat with mid-morning coffee, a little something after your lunchtime sandwich, an indulgence to go with a cup of afternoon tea, a post-dinner dessert, or a little midnight feast before bed. And whatever time you bring them out, you will always be greeted with smiles of pleasure. Everyone loves a cupcake – and every time of day seems to be a cupcake time of day.

Simple pleasures

Cupcakes are fun to bake because they're just so easy. They require basic ingredients and equipment, and they take very little time to bake. The only thing that might take a little time is the decoration and even that is up to you. Some of the sweetest, prettiest cupcakes are the simplest after all. A spoonful of white glacé icing and a single raspberry or glacé cherry can look stunning – and can take no time at all. And although a sophisticated cupcake piled with a more complex frosting, chocolate curls and chopped nuts might take a little longer, the result is so spectacular that you'll never mind putting in the extra effort.

Fun for adults, fun for kids

It's not just adults who can enjoy making and eating cupcakes. Kids can have a great time with them too. For younger children, you might want to make the cakes and frostings, then let the kids run wild sticking on plenty of decorations. Meanwhile, for older children, making, baking and decorating the cakes under supervision will be a rewarding challenge – and a great activity for a rainy afternoon. Weighing, measuring, timing and basic kitchen safety are all great skills to learn. Cooking with your kids is also a great way to have proper family time and really bond with them. Start them off with simpler recipes such as Passion Fruit Butterfly Cakes (pages 40–41) and Creamy Coconut Cupcakes (pages 26–27), or recipes from the Kids' Cupcakes chapter (pages 128–155).

The great thing about baking cupcakes is that the equipment required is basic. The techniques are generally simple and you'll only need the bare kitchen essentials to be able to rustle up the most professional-looking sugary creations imaginable.

equipment

An oven
An essential for baking – but whether it's gas or electric is unimportant. Some ovens have hotspots, and some cook quicker than others, but as you get to know your own oven, you'll know whether you need to turn the cupcake tin partway through baking to ensure evenly browned and risen cakes, or whether you'll need a minute or so less or more on the cooking time.

Measuring equipment
Quantities are all important when baking cakes and using the wrong proportions of ingredients can lead to disappointing results – or even failure. So make sure you have a set of accurate weighing scales, cups and spoons.

Sieves
A large sieve is invaluable for sifting dry ingredients such as flour and icing sugar before mixing, but a small sieve is also useful for dusting finished cakes with sugar.

Bowls and spoons
You only need the most basic equipment to beat together most cupcake mixtures. Although you can use an electric mixer if you prefer, as long as your butter is soft, it's just as easy to use an old-fashioned bowl and wooden spoon.

Cupcake tins
The easiest way to make cupcakes is to bake them in cupcake tins, which usually have six or 12 cup-shaped holes. For the prettiest effect, line them with paper cases before filling with cake mixture. However, they can simply be greased if you prefer. As well as standard cupcake tins, you can also find mini-cupcake and giant muffin tins.

Paper cupcake cases
When it comes to baking cupcakes, this is where the real fun begins. There are so many different types of pretty cupcake cases to slip inside your cupcake tins. You can find them in supermarkets and kitchen shops (see page 157) and they come in a fabulous array of colours and sizes. You can find plain white, pale pastel or brightly coloured ones, or pretty floral patterns, brightly coloured stripes, fun jungle prints, footballs for boys, or lovehearts for Valentine's Day. There are shiny metallic cases, too – gold, silver and plain colours, or stripes, spots and zigzags. There really is no end to the choice out there!

Timers
Like measuring equipment, timing is all important when it comes to baking so it's worth investing in a kitchen timer. You can use a clock or a watch, but it's all too easy to forget about the cakes in the oven and find you've over-baked them if you haven't got a little bell to remind you to go and check on them.

Wire racks
Cupcakes should usually be transferred from the baking tin to a wire rack to cool.

ingredients

Although there are many variations on the classic cupcake, most cupcake mixtures are based on four basic ingredients: butter, sugar, eggs and flour. Other ingredients such as chocolate, nuts, dried fruit and other flavourings such as vanilla and grated lemon zest may then be stirred through the mixture to add texture and flavour.

Butter

For the best results, it is usually best to use unsalted butter for cupcakes. For creamed mixtures, where the butter and sugar are beaten together, the butter should be left at room temperature until soft. For people with a dairy intolerance or allergy, they may prefer to use a non-dairy margarine in place of butter.

Sugar

The most common sugar for making cupcakes is caster sugar, but other sugars and sweeteners may also be used, all of which add their own unique taste and texture. Soft brown sugars, honey and syrups such as maple syrup will all add a distinctive flavour as well as sweetness to cakes. They will also affect the texture of the cakes. Honey and syrups are frequently heated before being used in cake mixtures such as the Gingerbread Cupcakes with Lemon Icing (pages 38–39).

Eggs

Used to enrich cakes, but also to bind the ingredients together, eggs are best used at room temperature. The eggs used in all the recipes in this book were medium.

Flour

Most cupcakes use self-raising flour or plain flour with a little baking powder to help the cakes rise. However, other flours can also be used to make cupcakes – either on their own or combined with self-raising or plain flour. Cornmeal, rice flour and potato flour are all popular. Ground almonds are also frequently used in place of flour in cupcakes.

Additional ingredients

There are countless additional ingredients that you can fold into a basic cupcake mixture.

Fruit is always popular – whether dried or fresh. Small dried fruits such as sultanas can be folded straight into the mixture, while larger fruits such as apricots will need to be chopped first. The same is true of fresh fruits. Blueberries and redcurrants can be folded in whole, while apples and pears should be peeled and chopped, and bananas might be mashed.

Nuts and seeds are other popular ingredients and may be added whole or chopped, depending on size. They add both flavour and texture.

You will also frequently use melted chocolate, marshmallows, coconut (desiccated, flaked and creamed), stem ginger and grated carrots.

Flavourings

There are many, many flavourings that may be added to cupcakes – and come in several forms including essences, ground spices, citrus zests and flavoured sugars. Particularly popular flavourings include vanilla, coffee, chocolate (cocoa or melted), spices such as cinnamon and ginger, lemon zest, rosewater, and liqueurs and spirits.

The way you choose to top your cupcakes really is where the fun begins – apart from eating them of course! And the decorations are so many and varied as to cause endless delight. Simple or sophisticated, plain or indulgent, there really is a choice to suit every taste. From the simplest dusting of icing sugar or drizzle of glacé icing, to swirls of rich buttercream, indulgent chocolate ganache, cool cream cheese frosting and all manner of goodies to sprinkle and scatter on top. The choices really are endless.

Keeping it simple

The simplest of all decorations is a light dusting of either icing sugar or cocoa powder. Cakes can also be decorated before baking with a sprinkling of flaked or chopped nuts, a little coarse sugar or perhaps a slice or two of fresh apple or a piece of dried fruit. Plain, undecorated cupcakes keep for 2–3 days in an airtight container, but cupcakes with icings, frostings or other embellishments should be eaten on the day.

Icings and frostings

Prettily coloured, sugary sweet icings and frostings that you can drizzle, spoon, swirl or pipe on top of cupcakes add a whole new dimension. Melted white or dark chocolate, or a glacé icing made from icing sugar and lemon juice are probably the simplest and are perfect for spooning or drizzling. Buttercreams, cream cheese frostings, chocolate ganaches, whipped cream and creamy custards are more indulgent and excellent for swirling and piping.

decorating and embellishments

Sprinkles, candies and other decorations

Once you've frosted your cupcake, you can leave it plain, but it's even more fun to add decorations. For simply decorated cakes, a whole nut, a glacé cherry or a brightly coloured sweet can look stunning stuck in the centre, right on top of a domed cupcake. But there are delightful coloured sugar sprinkles that you can scatter all over frosted cakes – from hundreds and thousands to tiny sugar shapes such as hearts, stars and flowers. Other decorations include sugar and rice paper flowers, gold and silver dragées, edible sparkles, firework sparklers that you can light at the table, party candles, cocktail decorations that are perfect for sticking into cakes, fresh berries and sugared rose petals. But look around. Supermarkets and kitchen shops are full of fabulous decorations and brightly coloured candies that are perfect for decorating cupcakes. Let your imagination run wild and don't be afraid to experiment with the food colouring when tinting your frosting.

Fondant fancies

Fondant icing, which can be bought ready-made and ready-to-roll from the supermarket, is perfect for making sophisticated, professional-looking cakes. The icing can be coloured with food colouring, then kneaded to incorporate the colouring, rolled out, cut into rounds and draped over cupcakes to give a silky smooth finish. Decorations can then be added – or more icing can be moulded into shapes to make funny faces such as the Pink Piggy Cupcakes (pages 130–131).

Cupcakes are so fabulously versatile. You can serve them with a cup of coffee or afternoon tea, bring them out for dessert after dinner, take them on a picnic, or offer them as a gift. There are just so many ways to serve cupcakes – and every way is always a hit.

A little sophistication

Whether you've invited friends round for morning coffee or afternoon tea, there's nothing more likely to have your guests 'ooing' and 'aaaaaahing' than a plateful of freshly baked, beautifully frosted cupcakes. Delicious cookies, fabulous cakes and luscious pastries pale into insignificance in the face of cupcakes, so forget about those other sweet treats and go for cupcakes every time! Lavender Cupcakes (pages 24–25), Blueberry and Lemon Cupcakes (pages 30–31), Maple and Pecan Cupcakes (pages 32–33) or pretty Spring Flower Cupcakes (pages 52–53) – whichever you choose, you know you'll be the hostess with the most!

Cute desserts

For dinner with friends, don't bother with the traditional approach of a big stodgy pudding or a fussy dessert – why not just bring out a plateful of cupcakes with coffee instead? It's so much easier for you as a hostess because you can prepare the cupcakes ahead. And your guests are guaranteed to be delighted when you bring out a mountain of adorable treats piled on one of the gorgeous cut-glass or pastel ceramic cake stands you can so easily find in shops now. You can even buy special cupcake stands for a truly extravagant display (see Suppliers and Stockists on page 157).

Cupcakes for kids

Children love cupcakes – making them, decorating them and eating them! So whether it's a lunchbox treat, a sugary something after school with a glass of milk, or a fantastic party piece for the birthday tea table, there really isn't a cupcake that children won't love. For younger children, serve up plainer cakes such as the Number Cupcakes (pages 132–133) or Vanilla Buttercream Cupcakes (pages 140–141) and for older ones try more sophisticated recipes such as Bird's Nest Cupcakes (pages 138–139), Chocolate Chip Cupcakes (pages 144–145) and Ice Cream Cupcakes (pages 148–149).

Cupcake gifts

Pretty cupcakes make wonderful gifts and are absolutely guaranteed to bring a smile to the face of the grateful recipient. Take them to a new mother to celebrate the birth of a child, or as a hostess gift when you're going to friends or family for a meal or to visit. Give them as a Valentine's gift or simply to say 'I love you'. Drop a batch round to a friend who's feeling blue, or to your mother just to let her know you care. Whatever the occasion, you'll always find that it's a cupcake occasion!

Pack them up in a single layer in a pretty box with clear plastic lids, or tuck them into a shallow basket, nestled into place with crumpled tissue paper. If you like, you can tie ribbons around each individual cake to add to the decorative effect.

SIMPLE CUPCAKES

Blackberry, apple and cinnamon are a sublime combination in these pretty little cakes. Studded with chunks of tender apple and warmly spiced with cinnamon, their moist, crumbly, melt-in-the-mouth taste and texture are offset perfectly by the sweet, sticky soured cream frosting.

APPLE AND CINNAMON CAKES

85 g unsalted butter, at room temperature

100 g caster sugar

1 egg, beaten

125 ml soured cream

150 g self-raising flour

¼ teaspoon bicarbonate of soda

½ teaspoon ground cinnamon

1 eating apple, peeled, cored and diced

to decorate

80 ml soured cream

about 100 g icing sugar, sifted

¼ teaspoon freshly squeezed lemon juice

about 36 blackberries

a 12-hole cupcake tin, lined with paper cases

makes 12

Preheat the oven to 180°C (350°F) Gas 4.

Beat the butter and sugar in a bowl until pale and creamy, then gradually beat in the egg. Stir in the soured cream. Combine the flour, bicarbonate of soda and cinnamon and sift into the mixture. Fold in, along with the apple.

Spoon the mixture into the paper cases and bake in the preheated oven for about 20 minutes until risen and golden and a skewer inserted in the centre comes out clean. Transfer to a wire rack to cool.

To decorate, put the soured cream and sugar in a bowl and beat together for about 1 minute until smooth and creamy. Add a little more sugar if the icing is not thick enough. Stir in the lemon juice. Spoon the icing on top of the cakes and top each one with two or three blackberries.

Lightly spiced and topped with a creamy citrus mascarpone frosting, these delightful little cakes are just the thing when you need a treat. They're not too sweet, but offer just the right combination of crunch, crumble, spice, sweetness and creaminess – plus that little hint of naughtiness that a cupcake should always have.

CARROT AND CARDAMOM CUPCAKES

100 g soft brown sugar

160 ml sunflower oil

2 eggs

grated zest of 1 unwaxed orange

seeds from 5 cardamom pods, crushed

½ teaspoon ground ginger

200 g self-raising flour

about 150 g carrot, grated

60 g shelled walnuts or pecan nuts, roughly chopped

to decorate

150 g mascarpone

finely grated zest of 1 unwaxed orange

1½ teaspoons freshly squeezed lemon juice

50 g icing sugar, sifted

a 12-hole cupcake tin, lined with paper cases

makes 12

Preheat the oven to 180°C (350°F) Gas 4.

Put the sugar in a bowl and break up using the back of a fork, then beat in the oil and eggs. Stir in the orange zest, crushed cardamom seeds and ginger, then sift the flour into the mixture and fold in, followed by the carrot and nuts.

Spoon the mixture into the paper cases and bake in the preheated oven for about 20 minutes until risen and a skewer inserted in the centre comes out clean. Transfer to a wire rack to cool.

To decorate, beat the mascarpone, orange zest, lemon juice and sugar together in a bowl and spread over the cakes.

Dense and almondy with a sticky, chewy marzipan centre, these sweet little cupcakes are reminiscent of an indulgent bakewell tart – but with a pretty paper case instead of a crisp pastry shell. Pack a few in a pretty box as a gift for a sweet-toothed friend and watch them disappear in no time.

CHERRY AND MARZIPAN CUPCAKES

115 g unsalted butter, at room temperature

115 g caster sugar

2 eggs

100 g self-raising flour

40 g ground almonds

60 g glacé cherries, quartered

25 g marzipan, finely grated

to decorate

2 tablespoons freshly squeezed lemon juice

200 g icing sugar, sifted

12 glacé cherries

a 12-hole cupcake tin, lined with paper cases

makes 12

Preheat the oven to 180°C (350°F) Gas 4.

Beat the butter and sugar together in a bowl until pale and fluffy, then beat in the eggs, one at a time. Sift the flour into the mixture and fold in, along with the ground almonds and glacé cherries.

Spoon small dollops of the mixture into the paper cases, sprinkle over some marzipan and top with the remaining mixture. Bake in the preheated oven for about 18 minutes until risen and golden and a skewer inserted in the centre comes out clean. Transfer to a wire rack to cool.

To decorate, put the lemon juice and sugar in a bowl and stir until smooth and creamy. Spoon on top of the cakes and top each one with a glacé cherry.

Subtly scented with lavender, these golden, buttery cupcakes are deliciously simple with an understated elegance, so they're perfect for serving mid-afternoon with a cup of tea. The fragrant taste of the lavender flowers gives the cakes an elusive hint that you can't quite put your finger on.

LAVENDER CUPCAKES

115 g caster sugar

¼ teaspoon dried lavender flowers

115 g unsalted butter, at room temperature

2 eggs

115 g self-raising flour

2 tablespoons milk

to decorate

185 g icing sugar, sifted

1 egg white

lilac food colouring

12 sprigs of fresh lavender

a 12-hole cupcake tin, lined with paper cases

makes 12

Preheat the oven to 180°C (350°F) Gas 4.

Put the sugar and lavender flowers in a food processor and process briefly to combine. Tip the lavender sugar into a bowl with the butter and beat together until pale and fluffy.

Beat the eggs into the butter mixture, one at a time, then sift in the flour and fold in. Stir in the milk.

Spoon the mixture into the paper cases. Bake in the preheated oven for about 18 minutes until risen and golden and a skewer inserted in the centre comes out clean. Transfer to a wire rack to cool.

To decorate, gradually beat the sugar into the egg white in a bowl, then add a few drops of food colouring and stir to achieve a lavender-coloured icing. Spoon the icing over the cakes, then top each one with a sprig of fresh lavender. Leave to set before serving.

Sweet with coconut and tangy with lime, these golden cakes with their snowy-white, ruffled tops look stunning arranged on a coloured plate. Serve them mid-morning with coffee, mid-afternoon with tea or after dinner as a simple dessert. They are deceptively easy to make and yet look so delightful that everyone will want to tuck in.

CREAMY COCONUT CUPCAKES

90 g unsalted butter, at room temperature

25 g creamed coconut

115 g caster sugar

2 eggs

100 g self-raising flour

1 teaspoon baking powder

25 g desiccated coconut

grated zest of 1 unwaxed lime

2 tablespoons milk

to decorate

150 g cream cheese

50 g icing sugar, sifted

2 teaspoons freshly squeezed lime juice

40 g coconut shavings

a 12-hole cupcake tin, lined with paper cases

makes 12

Preheat the oven to 180°C (350°F) Gas 4.

Beat the butter, creamed coconut and sugar together in a bowl until pale and fluffy, then beat in the eggs, one at a time. Sift the flour and baking powder into the mixture and fold in, then stir in the desiccated coconut and lime zest, followed by the milk.

Spoon the mixture into the paper cases, then bake in the preheated oven for about 17 minutes until risen and golden and a skewer inserted in the centre comes out clean. Transfer to a wire rack to cool.

To decorate, beat the cream cheese, sugar and lime juice together in a bowl. Swirl the frosting on top of the cakes, then sprinkle over the coconut shavings in a thick layer.

Orange and poppyseed are a classic combination in these lusciously simple, tangy cupcakes. The luxuriously creamy mascarpone topping adds just the right edge of indulgence to the delicate citrus sponge speckled with tiny black poppyseeds. You might even convince yourself that these were fruity enough to have for breakfast!

ORANGE AND POPPYSEED CUPCAKES

115 g unsalted butter, at room temperature

115 g caster sugar

2 eggs

115 g self-raising flour

finely grated zest of 1 unwaxed orange

1 tablespoon poppyseeds

to decorate

2 oranges

a 250-g tub of mascarpone

85 g icing sugar, sifted

a 12-hole cupcake tin, lined with paper cases

makes 12

Preheat the oven to 180°C (350°F) Gas 4.

Beat the butter and sugar together in a bowl until pale and fluffy, then beat in the eggs one at a time. Sift the flour into the mixture and fold in, then stir in the orange zest and poppyseeds.

Spoon the mixture into the paper cases and bake in the preheated oven for about 18 minutes until risen and golden and a skewer inserted into the centre comes out clean. Transfer to a wire rack to cool.

To decorate, finely grate the zest from one of the oranges and set the zest aside. Put both the oranges on a chopping board and slice off the peel and white pith. Cut between the membranes to remove the orange segments, then set aside.

Put the mascarpone, sugar and reserved orange zest in a bowl and beat together until smooth and creamy. Swirl the frosting on top of the cakes, then decorate with orange segments.

Using golden polenta gives these cakes a distinctive texture with an almost crispy bite and a gloriously rich colour. Studded with juicy blueberries and topped with a rich, zesty cream cheese frosting, they offer the perfect pairing of light, fresh fruit and rich, creamy indulgence. Mouth-watering!

BLUEBERRY AND LEMON CUPCAKES

50 g polenta

40 g plain flour

1 teaspoon baking powder

1 tablespoon crème fraîche

1½ tablespoons sunflower oil

grated zest of 1 unwaxed lemon

1 tablespoon freshly squeezed lemon juice

1 egg

50 g caster sugar

60 g blueberries

to decorate

150 g cream cheese

100 g icing sugar, sifted

½ teaspoon grated unwaxed lemon zest

1 tablespoon freshly squeezed lemon juice

about 60 g blueberries

strips of unwaxed lemon zest

a 12-hole cupcake tin, lined with just 10 paper cases

makes 10

Preheat the oven to 180°C (350°F) Gas 4.

Combine the polenta, flour and baking powder in a bowl, then set aside. Beat the crème fraîche, oil, lemon zest and juice together in a jug, then set aside.

In a separate bowl, whisk the egg and sugar together for about 4 minutes until thick and pale, then add the lemon mixture and fold in. Sift the polenta mixture over the top and fold in to combine.

Spoon the mixture into the paper cases, then drop about 4 blueberries on top of each one, gently pressing them into the mixture. Bake in the preheated oven for 15–16 minutes until risen and golden and a skewer inserted in the centre comes out clean. Transfer to a wire rack to cool.

To decorate, beat the cream cheese in a bowl until creamy, then beat in the sugar, lemon zest and juice. Swirl big dollops of frosting on top of the cakes and decorate with fresh blueberries and strips of lemon zest.

Maple syrup and pecans are a classic combination, and no better anywhere than in these light, sticky cakes topped with creamy, buttery frosting and caramelized pecans. Look out for the darker, amber maple syrup as it has a more intense flavour that really shines through in the fluffy, buttery sponge.

MAPLE AND PECAN CUPCAKES

115 g unsalted butter, at room temperature

50 g soft brown sugar

160 ml maple syrup

2 eggs

115 g self-raising flour

60 g shelled pecan nuts, roughly chopped

to decorate

60 g caster sugar

12 pecan nut halves

50 g unsalted butter, at room temperature

3 tablespoons maple syrup

145 g icing sugar, sifted

a 12-hole cupcake tin, lined with paper cases

makes 12

Preheat the oven to 180°C (350°F) Gas 4.

Beat the butter and sugar together in a bowl until creamy, then beat in the maple syrup. Beat in the eggs, one at a time, then sift the flour into the mixture and fold in, along with the nuts.

Spoon the mixture into the paper cases and bake in the preheated oven for about 17 minutes until risen and golden and a skewer inserted in the centre comes out clean. Transfer to a wire rack to cool.

To make the caramelized pecans, put the caster sugar in a saucepan and add 2 tablespoons water. Heat gently, stirring, until the sugar melts and dissolves. Increase the heat and boil for about 6 minutes until it turns a pale gold colour. Spread the nuts out on a sheet of greaseproof paper and spoon over a little of the caramel to cover each nut individually. Leave to cool.

Beat the butter, maple syrup and icing sugar together in a bowl until pale and fluffy. Spread the mixture over the cakes and top each one with a caramelized pecan.

Delicately scented with rosewater, these gorgeous pink cupcakes are perfect for girls who like things extra-pretty. I like pale pink sugared rose petals on mine, but darker pink or white will look just as lovely. For an extra indulgence, try stirring 75 g chopped Turkish delight into the cake mixture before spooning it into the paper cases.

ROSEWATER CUPCAKES

115 g unsalted butter, at room temperature

115 g caster sugar

2 eggs

115 g self-raising flour

1 tablespoon rosewater

to decorate

12 pink rose petals

1 egg white, beaten

1 tablespoon caster sugar

1½–2 tablespoons freshly squeezed lemon juice

145 g icing sugar, sifted

pink food colouring

a 12-hole cupcake tin, lined with paper cases

makes 12

Preheat the oven to 180°C (350°F) Gas 4.

Beat the butter and sugar together in a bowl until pale and fluffy, then beat in the eggs, one at a time. Sift the flour into the mixture and fold in, then stir in the rosewater.

Spoon the mixture into the paper cases and bake in the preheated oven for about 17 minutes until risen and golden and a skewer inserted in the centre comes out clean. Transfer to a wire rack to cool.

To decorate, brush each rose petal with egg white, then sprinkle with the caster sugar and leave to dry for about 1 hour.

Put 1½ tablespoons lemon juice in a bowl, then sift the icing sugar into the bowl and stir until smooth. Add a little more lemon juice as required to make a smooth, spoonable icing. Add one or two drops of food colouring to achieve a pale pink icing, then spread over the cakes. Top each one with a sugared rose petal. Leave to set before serving.

These sweet, sticky, crumbly cakes are divine and make a sophisticated alternative to the classic iced cupcake. They're particularly good served with a cup of fragrant tea such as jasmine, Earl Grey or Lapsang Souchong. Make sure they are still warm when you serve them to enjoy them at their very best.

APRICOT, HONEY AND PINE NUT CUPCAKES

75 g unsalted butter

40 g light brown sugar

60 ml clear honey

½ tablespoon milk

1 egg

100 g self-raising flour

25 g ready-to-eat dried apricots, roughly chopped

2 tablespoons pine nuts

to decorate

4 tablespoons pine nuts, toasted

50 g ready-to-eat dried apricots, roughly chopped

4 tablespoons clear honey

a 12-hole cupcake tin, lined with just 10 paper cases

makes 10

Preheat the oven to 180°C (350°F) Gas 4.

Put the butter, sugar, honey and milk in a saucepan and warm over very gentle heat, stirring occasionally until melted. Remove from the heat and leave to cool for 5 minutes.

Beat the egg into the warm mixture, then stir in the flour. Fold in the apricots and pine nuts.

Spoon the mixture into the paper cases and bake in the preheated oven for 15 minutes until risen and golden and a skewer inserted in the centre comes out clean. Transfer to a wire rack.

To decorate, put the pine nuts, apricots and honey in a small saucepan and warm gently over low heat. Stir until the honey has melted and the apricots and pine nuts are well coated. Spoon the mixture over the cakes and serve warm.

These soft, sticky, dark brown cakes are dense and gingery, and delicious drizzled with a simple lemon icing. If you want elegant flat-topped cakes, make them in large cupcake cases, but if you prefer domed cakes with icing drizzling down the sides, make them in regular-sized cases.

GINGERBREAD CUPCAKES WITH LEMON ICING

60 g unsalted butter

50 g soft brown sugar

2 tablespoons golden syrup

2 tablespoons black treacle

1 teaspoon ground ginger

80 ml milk

1 egg, beaten

2 pieces of stem ginger in syrup, drained and chopped

115 g self-raising flour

to decorate

2 tablespoons freshly squeezed lemon juice

200 g icing sugar, sifted

2–3 pieces of stem ginger in syrup, drained and chopped

a 12-hole cupcake tin, lined with paper cases

makes 12

Preheat the oven to 170°C (325°F) Gas 3.

Put the butter, sugar, golden syrup, treacle and ground ginger in a saucepan and heat gently until melted. Remove the pan from the heat and stir in the milk, then beat in the egg and stem ginger. Sift the flour into the mixture and fold in.

Spoon the mixture into the paper cases and bake in the preheated oven for about 20 minutes until risen and a skewer inserted in the centre comes out clean. Transfer to a wire rack to cool.

To decorate, pour the lemon juice into a bowl. Gradually sift in the sugar, stirring as you go, until smooth, thick and spoonable. Spoon the icing over the cakes and put a few pieces of stem ginger on each one. Leave to set before serving.

A plateful of these pretty, passion fruit-scented cakes look like a swarm of fluttering butterflies. They remind me of the children's tea parties of my youth, where you were guaranteed to find a batch of butterfly cakes clustered on the tea table. So these are perfect for the child in us all!

PASSION FRUIT BUTTERFLY CAKES

3 passion fruit

115 g unsalted butter,
at room temperature

115 g caster sugar

2 eggs

115 g self-raising flour

1 teaspoon baking powder

to decorate

6 passion fruit

150 g mascarpone

4 tablespoons icing sugar, sifted,
plus extra to dust

*a 12-hole cupcake tin,
lined with paper cases*

makes 12

Preheat the oven to 180°C (350°F) Gas 4.

Halve the passion fruit and scoop the flesh into a sieve set over a bowl. Press with the back of a teaspoon to extract the juice.

Beat the butter and sugar together in a bowl until pale and fluffy, then beat in the eggs, one at a time. Sift the flour and baking powder into the mixture and fold in. Stir in the passion fruit juice.

Spoon the mixture into the paper cases, then bake in the preheated oven for about 17 minutes until risen and golden and a skewer inserted in the centre comes out clean. Transfer to a wire rack to cool.

To decorate, halve the passion fruit and scoop the flesh into a sieve set over a bowl. Press with the back of a teaspoon to extract the juice, then add the mascarpone and sugar to the bowl. Mix until smooth and creamy. Cover and refrigerate for about 30 minutes to thicken up.

Slice the top off each cake, then cut each top in half. Spoon a generous dollop of the mascarpone mixture onto each cake, then top with the two halves, setting them at an angle to resemble wings. Dust with icing sugar and serve.

With a pale green crumb and a subtle taste of pistachio, these little cupcakes are utterly irresistible and unbelievably girly (which is just the way they should be)! To achieve a pale pistachio-coloured icing, use a light green food colouring if you can find one, adding a little at a time until you achieve just the right shade.

PISTACHIO CUPCAKES

45 g shelled pistachio nuts

115 g unsalted butter, at room temperature

115 g caster sugar

2 eggs

100 g self-raising flour

2 tablespoons milk

to decorate

1 egg white

185 g icing sugar

¾ teaspoon freshly squeezed lemon juice

green food colouring

12 pink rice paper roses

a 12-hole cupcake tin, lined with paper cases

makes 12

Preheat the oven to 180°C (350°F) Gas 4.

Put the pistachio nuts in a food processor and process until finely ground. Set aside.

Beat the butter and sugar together in a bowl until pale and fluffy, then beat in the eggs, one at a time. Stir in the ground nuts, then sift the flour into the mixture and fold in. Stir in the milk.

Spoon the mixture into the paper cases. Bake in the preheated oven for about 18 minutes until risen and golden and a skewer inserted in the centre comes out clean. Transfer to a wire rack to cool.

To decorate, put the egg white in a bowl and gradually sift over the sugar, beating in as you go until thick and glossy, then beat in the lemon juice. The icing should be thick but spoonable.

Add a few drops of food colouring to the icing and beat to make a pale pistachio-green icing. Spoon on top of the cakes and top each one with a pink rice paper rose. Leave to set before serving.

CELEBRATION
CUPCAKES

Who wants an old-fashioned tiered wedding cake when you could have a mountain of these pretty white wedding cupcakes instead? I like the white look when it comes to the decorations, but you can add pastel food colouring, flowers or ribbon according to your colour scheme. You can also use larger muffin tins to make a variety of sizes.

WEDDING CUPCAKES

115 g unsalted butter, at room temperature

115 g caster sugar

2 eggs

115 g self-raising flour

1 teaspoon vanilla extract or grated unwaxed lemon zest

2 tablespoons milk

to decorate

white lace or organza ribbon

1 egg white

125 g icing sugar, sifted

½ teaspoon freshly squeezed lemon juice

white edible flower decorations

a 12-hole cupcake tin, lined with paper cases

makes 12

Preheat the oven to 180°C (350°F) Gas 4.

Beat the butter and sugar together in a bowl until pale and fluffy, then beat in the eggs, one at a time. Sift the flour into the mixture and fold in. Stir in the vanilla extract or lemon zest and the milk.

Spoon the mixture into the paper cases and bake in the preheated oven for about 18 minutes until risen and golden and a skewer inserted in the centre comes out clean. Transfer to a wire rack to cool.

To decorate, carefully tie a piece of ribbon around each cake. Put the egg white in a large bowl, then beat in the sugar until thick and creamy. Beat in the lemon juice to make a thick, spoonable icing. (If necessary, add a drizzle more lemon juice or a little more sugar to get the right consistency.)

Spoon the icing onto the cakes, then top each one with a flower. The icing hardens quite fast, so work quickly as soon as you've made the icing.

These rich chocolate cupcakes are the wickedly indulgent antithesis of the traditional white wedding cake – the only choice for the passionate chocaholic who finds themselves walking up the aisle. For the perfect result, use the best-quality dark chocolate and the most gorgeous dark crimson rose you can find.

DARK CHOCOLATE WEDDING CUPCAKES

75 g dark chocolate, chopped

85 g unsalted butter, at room temperature

115 g caster sugar

2 eggs

3 tablespoons crème fraîche

115 g self-raising flour

1 tablespoon Grand Marnier

to decorate

100 ml double cream

100 g dark chocolate, finely chopped

a dark crimson rose

a 12-hole cupcake tin, lined with paper cases

makes 12

Preheat the oven to 180°C (350°F) Gas 4.

Put the chocolate in a heatproof bowl set over a pan of gently simmering water. Do not let the bowl touch the water. Leave until almost melted. Remove from the heat and leave to cool for about 5 minutes.

In a clean bowl, beat together the butter and sugar until pale and creamy, then beat in the eggs, one at a time. Stir in the crème fraîche, then sift the flour into the mixture and fold in. Stir in the melted chocolate, followed by the Grand Marnier.

Spoon the mixture into the paper cases and bake in the preheated oven for 18 minutes until risen and a skewer inserted in the centre comes out clean. Transfer to a wire rack to cool.

To decorate, gently heat the cream until almost boiling, then pour over the chopped chocolate and leave to melt for about 5 minutes. Stir until the chocolate has melted, then refrigerate for 20–30 minutes. Beat until thick and glossy, then spoon on top of the cakes.

Hold the rose head gently but firmly in one hand, and twist off away from the stem, then carefully separate the petals. Decorate each cake with a perfect rose petal.

These sparkling cupcakes are perfect for an engagement party – or any celebration! Or for the true romantic, why not whip up a batch ready to propose with? Choose any shade of food colouring you like for the icing and you can adapt these cupcakes to suit any number of glamorous occasions.

SPARKLING DIAMOND CUPCAKES

115 g unsalted butter, at room temperature

115 g caster sugar

2 eggs

115 g self-raising flour

3 pieces of stem ginger in syrup, drained and chopped

grated zest of 1 unwaxed lime

to decorate

about 6 clear mints

2½ tablespoons freshly squeezed lime juice

200 g icing sugar, sifted

pale blue food colouring

edible clear sparkles

a 12-hole cupcake tin, lined with silver paper cases

makes 12

Preheat the oven to 180°C (350°F) Gas 4.

Beat the butter and sugar together in a bowl until pale and fluffy, then beat in the eggs, one at a time. Sift the flour into the mixture and fold in, then stir in the ginger and lime zest.

Spoon the mixture into the paper cases, then bake in the preheated oven for about 17 minutes until risen and golden and a skewer inserted in the centre comes out clean. Transfer to a wire rack and leave to cool completely.

To decorate, leave the mints in their wrapper and tap with a rolling pin to break into pieces. Set aside.

Put the lime juice in a bowl, then sift the icing sugar into the bowl and stir until smooth. Add a little more lime juice as required to make a smooth, spoonable icing. Add a couple of drops of food colouring and stir in to achieve a pale blue colour.

Spoon the icing on top of the cakes. Pile a little heap of mint 'diamonds' on each cake and sprinkle with edible sparkles.

These pretty floral cakes are perfect for welcoming in the beginning of spring, the warmer weather and the arrival of spring flowers. You could also offer them as a gift for Mother's Day or Easter. You can find plenty of simple sugar flower decorations in most supermarkets, but search out kitchen shops for a wider selection.

SPRING FLOWER CUPCAKES

115 g unsalted butter, at room temperature

115 g caster sugar

2 eggs

115 g self-raising flour

1 teaspoon vanilla extract

2 tablespoons milk

to decorate

2 egg whites

350 g icing sugar, sifted

2½ teaspoons freshly squeezed lemon juice

green food colouring

yellow food colouring

12 sugar spring flowers, such as daffodils or daisies

a 12-hole cupcake tin, lined with paper cases

makes 12

Preheat the oven to 180°C (350°F) Gas 4.

Beat the butter and sugar together in a bowl until pale and fluffy, then beat in the eggs, one at a time. Sift the flour into the mixture and fold in, then stir in the vanilla extract and milk.

Spoon the mixture into the paper cases and bake in the preheated oven for about 15 minutes until risen and golden and a skewer inserted in the centre comes out clean. Transfer to a wire rack to cool. If any of the cakes have risen above the level of the paper case, slice off the top using a serrated knife to create a flat surface.

To decorate, put the egg whites in a bowl and gradually beat in the sugar, then the lemon juice, to give a thick, glossy, spoonable icing.

Divide the icing between two bowls and tint one with green food colouring and the other with yellow to create pretty, fresh pastel shades. Spoon the icing over the cakes — it should naturally spread to the edges of the paper cases. If any air bubbles appear, gently prick with a cocktail stick, then top each cake with a sugar flower. The icing will firm up and set within 1 hour.

Valentine's day, a romantic dessert, or just because you love someone... These gorgeous little cakes with the wonderful combination of tart redcurrants, sweet vanilla and luscious, indulgent cream cheese frosting are the loveliest way to tell someone how you really feel about them. Decorate with the prettiest sparkles you can find.

PURPLE PASSION CUPCAKES

115 g unsalted butter,
at room temperature

115 g caster sugar

2 eggs

115 g self-raising flour

½ teaspoon vanilla extract

100 g redcurrants

to decorate

150 g cream cheese

60 g icing sugar, sifted

¼ teaspoon vanilla extract

violet food colouring

12 small sprigs of redcurrants

12 silver chocolate hearts

edible clear sparkles

*a 12-hole cupcake tin,
lined with paper cases*

makes 12

Preheat the oven to 180°C (350°F) Gas 4.

Beat the butter and sugar until pale and fluffy, then beat in the eggs, one at a time. Sift the flour in the mixture and fold in, then stir in the vanilla extract. Sprinkle over the redcurrants and gently fold in.

Spoon the mixture into the paper cases and bake in the preheated oven for 18 minutes until risen and golden and a skewer inserted in the centre comes out clean. Transfer to a wire rack to cool.

To decorate, put the cream cheese, sugar and vanilla extract in a bowl and beat together until smooth and creamy. Add a few drops of the food colouring and beat together to make a violet frosting.

Swirl the frosting on the cakes, then top each one with a small sprig of redcurrants and a silver chocolate heart. Sprinkle with edible sparkles.

Bake a batch of these delightfully flirtatious cakes filled with a zesty lemon cream and fresh raspberries for the one you love, and they'll never have eyes for anyone but you! For that extra-special touch, buy a cupcake tin with heart-shaped holes and push your regular paper cases into the holes.

RASPBERRY LOVE-HEART CUPCAKES

115 g unsalted butter, at room temperature

115 g caster sugar

2 eggs

115 g self-raising flour

grated zest and freshly squeezed juice of ½ unwaxed lemon

to decorate

80 ml crème fraîche

1 tablespoon good-quality lemon curd

60 g raspberries

icing sugar, for dusting

a 12-hole cupcake tin (with heart-shaped holes if you can find one), lined with paper cases

a mini heart-shaped cookie cutter

makes 12

Preheat the oven to 180°C (350°F) Gas 4.

Beat the butter and sugar together in a bowl until pale and fluffy, then beat in the eggs, one at a time. Sift the flour into the mixture and fold in, then stir in the lemon zest and juice.

Spoon the mixture into the paper cases and bake in the preheated oven for about 18 minutes until risen and golden and a skewer inserted in the centre comes out clean. Transfer to a wire rack to cool.

To decorate, using a sharp, pointed knife, remove a deep round from the centre of each cake, about 3 cm in diameter. Slice the pointed bit off each piece of cored-out cake so that you are left with a disc. Using the mini heart-shaped cookie cutter, cut the discs into hearts.

Combine the crème fraîche and lemon curd in a bowl, then fold in the raspberries. Spoon the mixture into the hollowed-out cakes, then top with the hearts. Dust with icing sugar.

Pears and cranberries are classic seasonal Christmas fruits and nowhere better than in these moist, lightly spiced cupcakes topped with a luscious brandy butter. If you're baking the cupcakes for people who don't like the taste of brandy, substitute milk for the brandy and add 1 teaspoon vanilla extract.

PEAR AND CRANBERRY CHRISTMAS CUPCAKES

60 g unsalted butter, at room temperature

115 g caster sugar

2 eggs

115 g self-raising flour

½ teaspoon mixed spice

1 pear, peeled, cored and diced

40 g dried cranberries

to decorate

100 g unsalted butter, at room temperature

150 g icing sugar, sifted

4 teaspoons brandy

about 36 fresh cranberries

12 small holly leaves (optional)

edible gold balls

a 12-hole cupcake tin, lined with paper cases

makes 12

Preheat the oven to 180°C (350°F) Gas 4.

Beat the butter and sugar together in a bowl until pale and fluffy, then beat in the eggs, one at a time. Sift the flour and mixed spice into the mixture and fold in, then stir in the pear and cranberries.

Spoon the mixture into the paper cases and bake in the preheated oven for about 18 minutes until risen and golden and a skewer inserted in the centre comes out clean. Transfer to a wire rack to cool.

To decorate, put the butter, sugar and brandy in a bowl and beat together until smooth and creamy. Swirl the frosting on top of the cakes, then decorate each one with two or three fresh cranberries, a holly leaf, if using, and sprinkle with edible balls.

These pretty cupcakes are just the thing to get you in the festive mood and the fruity buns are much lighter than traditional Christmas cake. Make the fondant stars the day before to let them firm up. If you can't find any blue fondant icing, add a few drops of blue food colouring to 100 g white fondant icing and knead to make a pale blue.

STARRY CHRISTMAS CUPCAKES

60 g unsalted butter, at room temperature

60 g soft brown sugar

1 egg

grated zest of 1 unwaxed orange

60 g self-raising flour

1 tablespoon brandy

4 ready-to-eat dried figs, chopped

25 g sultanas

70 g glacé cherries, halved

to decorate

100 g blue ready-to-roll fondant icing

350 g icing sugar, sifted

3 egg whites

2½ teaspoons freshly squeezed lemon juice

edible silver balls

edible clear sparkles

a mini star-shaped cookie cutter

a 12-hole cupcake tin, lined with paper cases

makes 12

Make the star decorations the day before you plan to make the cakes. Roll out the fondant icing, then use the cookie cutter to cut out 12 stars. Set aside and leave to dry overnight.

To make the cupcakes, preheat the oven to 180°C (350°F) Gas 4.

Beat the butter and sugar together in a bowl until creamy, then gradually beat in the egg, followed by the orange zest. Sift the flour into the mixture and fold in, then stir in the brandy, followed by the dried fruit and glacé cherries.

Spoon the mixture into the paper cases and bake in the preheated oven for about 14 minutes until risen and golden and a skewer inserted in the centre comes out clean. Transfer to a wire rack to cool.

To decorate, gradually whisk the sugar into 2 of the egg whites in a bowl until smooth and creamy, then beat in the lemon juice. Spoon the mixture over the cakes and scatter over the silver balls. Leave to firm up slightly.

Place the star decorations on top of the cakes, brush with the remaining egg white and sprinkle with edible sparkles.

Sweet, spicy pumpkin cakes topped with pretty white and dark chocolate cobwebs are definitely a treat rather than a trick. You can leave the topping to set completely if you like, but they're so much better when it's still soft. Around October you should be able to find spooky paper cases in specialist kitchen shops.

HALLOWEEN CUPCAKES

115 g soft brown sugar

120 ml sunflower oil

2 eggs

115 g pumpkin or butternut squash flesh, grated

grated zest of 1 unwaxed lemon

115 g self-raising flour

1 teaspoon baking powder

1 teaspoon ground cinnamon

to decorate

150 g white chocolate, chopped

25 g dark chocolate

a 12-hole cupcake tin, lined with paper cases

makes 12

Preheat the oven to 180°C (350°F) Gas 4.

Put the sugar in a bowl and break up with the back of a fork, then beat in the oil and eggs. Fold in the grated pumpkin and lemon zest. Combine the flour, baking powder and cinnamon in a bowl, then sift into the mixture and fold in.

Spoon the mixture into the paper cases and bake in the preheated oven for about 18 minutes until risen and a skewer inserted in the centre comes out clean. Transfer to a wire rack to cool.

To decorate, put the white and dark chocolates in separate heatproof bowls set over pans of gently simmering water. Do not let the bowls touch the water. Leave until almost melted. Remove from the heat and leave to cool for about 5 minutes, then spoon the white chocolate over the cakes.

Cut a large square of greaseproof paper and fold into eighths to make a cone and tape together. Spoon the dark chocolate into the cone and snip the tip off so that you can pipe a thin line of chocolate. Put a dot of chocolate in the centre of each cake, then pipe three concentric circles around the dot.

Using a skewer, draw a line from the central dot to the outside edge of the cake and repeat about eight times all the way round to create a spider's web pattern. Serve while the chocolate is still slightly soft and gooey.

These cute little peanut-flavoured cakes filled with a blob of fruity jam are just perfect for the big kid in us all. Look out for shiny, foil cupcake cases to add some extra sparkle. They make great mini-desserts for a birthday dinner party – just remember to warn everyone that they contain peanuts in case anyone is allergic to them.

PEANUT BUTTER AND RASPBERRY JELLY PARTYCAKES

60 g unsalted butter, at room temperature

60 g crunchy peanut butter

115 g caster sugar

2 eggs

115 g self-raising flour

2 tablespoons raspberry or strawberry jam

to decorate

3 tablespoons smooth peanut butter

4 tablespoons mascarpone

50 g icing sugar, sifted

edible gold balls

candles (optional)

a 12-hole cupcake tin, lined with foil cases

makes 12

Preheat the oven to 180°C (350°F) Gas 4.

Beat the butter, peanut butter and sugar together in a bowl until pale and fluffy, then beat in the eggs, one at a time. Sift the flour into the mixture and fold in.

Spoon dollops of the mixture into the foil cases and flatten slightly with the back of a teaspoon, making a slight indent in the centre. Drop about ½ teaspoon jam in the centre of each indent. Top with the remaining cake mixture. Bake in the preheated oven for about 18 minutes until risen and golden. Transfer to a wire rack and leave to cool completely.

To decorate the cakes, put the peanut butter and mascarpone in a bowl and stir to combine, then stir in the sugar until smooth and creamy. Swirl the frosting on top of the cakes and sprinkle with edible balls. Pop a candle in each cake, if using.

You'll never want a traditional birthday cake again after sampling these gooey, chocolatey and nutty baby brownie cakes. Choose any nuts you like – macadamia nuts add a lovely buttery taste. Put the cupcakes on a cake stand or plate and gently press a candle into each one. Turn out the lights, light the candles and voilà!

CHOCOLATE BROWNIE BIRTHDAY CUPCAKES

75 g dark chocolate, chopped

75 g unsalted butter

1 egg

75 g caster sugar

25 g self-raising flour

50 g shelled macadamia nuts, pecan nuts or walnuts, coarsely chopped

12 mini-candles

two mini-cupcake tins, lined with petits fours cases

makes 18

Preheat the oven to 180°C (350°F) Gas 4.

Put the chocolate and butter in a heatproof bowl set over a pan of gently simmering water. Do not let the bowl touch the water. Stir until almost melted. Remove from the heat and leave to cool for about 5 minutes.

Beat in the egg, then stir in the sugar. Sift the flour into the mixture and fold in, then stir in the nuts.

Spoon the mixture into the petits fours cases and bake in the preheated oven for about 17 minutes until the top has turned pale and crackly and is just firm to the touch. Transfer to a wire rack to cool, before serving with a glowing candle in the centre of each one.

These cute little chocolate cupcakes with a feathered cream cheese and toffee frosting are smart and indulgent. With their marble sponge and dulce de leche topping, children will love them as much as adults. Look out for dulce de leche sold in squeezy bottles as it makes drizzling so much easier (see page 105).

MARBLE CUPCAKES

115 g unsalted butter, at room temperature

115 g caster sugar

2 eggs

115 g self-raising flour

1 tablespoon cocoa powder

to decorate

150 g cream cheese

50 g icing sugar, sifted

2 tablespoons double cream

dulce de leche, for drizzling

a 12-hole cupcake tin, lined with paper cases

makes 12

Preheat the oven to 180°C (350°F) Gas 4.

Beat the butter and sugar together in a bowl until pale and fluffy, then beat in the eggs, one at a time. Sift the flour into the mixture and fold in, then divide the mixture between two bowls. Add the cocoa powder to one bowl and stir in.

Drop alternating teaspoonfuls of the two cake mixtures into the paper cases. Using a skewer, cut through the mixture a couple of times to marble it, then bake the cakes in the preheated oven for 17 minutes until risen and golden and a skewer inserted in the centre comes out clean. Transfer to a wire rack to cool.

To decorate, put the cream cheese and sugar in a bowl and beat together until smooth and creamy, then stir in the cream to make a smooth, creamy frosting. Spread the frosting over the cakes, then squirt lines of dulce de leche over the top. Leave as they are, or draw a skewer through the dulce de leche to give a feathered effect.

For their sheer cuteness alone, these pastel-coloured mini-cupcakes are irresistible. Bake up a batch as a gift for a new mother to celebrate the arrival of her newborn. The white chocolate topping sets, so they're ideal for packing up in a pretty gift box – and just the treat she'll need to get her through those first few sleepless nights.

VANILLA AND WHITE CHOCOLATE BABYCAKES

60 g unsalted butter, at room temperature

60 g caster sugar

1 egg, beaten

60 g self-raising flour

¼ teaspoon vanilla extract

1 tablespoon milk

to decorate

60 g white chocolate, chopped

green food colouring

pink food colouring

15 pastel-coloured candies

a 12-hole mini-cupcake tin or a baking sheet, plus 12 petits fours cases

makes 12

Preheat the oven to 180°C (350°F) Gas 4, then line the mini-cupcake tin with petit fours cases. (If you don't have a mini-cupcake tin, arrange the cases on a baking sheet; the cases should be able to cope with such a small amount of mixture.)

Beat the butter and sugar together in a bowl until pale and fluffy, then beat in the egg, a little at a time. Sift the flour into the mixture and fold in, then stir in the vanilla extract and milk.

Spoon the mixture into the petits fours cases, then bake in the preheated oven for about 15 minutes until risen and golden and the tops spring back when gently pressed. Transfer to a wire rack to cool.

To decorate, divide the chocolate among three heatproof bowls and set over pans of gently simmering water. Do not let the bowls touch the water. Leave until almost melted. Leave to cool slightly, then stir a couple of drops of green food colouring into one bowl of chocolate and a couple of drops of pink into another. Leave the third bowl of chocolate plain.

Spoon white chocolate over four of the cakes, pink over another four and green over the remaining four, then top each one with a candy. Serve while the chocolate is still soft, or leave to set and package up as a gift.

These pretty, lemony, pastel-coloured babycakes are perfect for serving at christenings or similar baby celebrations. Because the cakes are small, it makes them ideal for older brothers and sisters to get their little hands round too. As this recipe makes 24 mini-cupcakes, use two mini-cupcake tins, or make them in two batches.

CHRISTENING CUPCAKES

115 g unsalted butter, at room temperature

115 g caster sugar

2 eggs

115 g self-raising flour

1½ teaspoons finely grated unwaxed lemon zest

to decorate

115 g cream cheese

75 g icing sugar, sifted

1¼ teaspoons freshly squeezed lemon juice

pink food colouring

blue food colouring

edible silver balls

a 12-hole mini-cupcake tin, lined with petits fours cases

makes 24

Preheat the oven to 180°C (350°F) Gas 4.

Beat the butter and sugar until pale and fluffy, then beat in the eggs, one at a time. Sift the flour into the mixture and fold in, then stir in the lemon zest.

Spoon the mixture into the petits fours cases, then bake in the preheated oven for about 15 minutes until risen and golden and a skewer inserted in the centre comes out clean. Transfer to a wire rack to cool completely.

To decorate, beat the cream cheese briefly until soft. Gradually beat in the sugar until smooth and creamy, then stir in the lemon juice. Divide the icing among two bowls, add a few drops of food colouring to each one and stir well to make baby pink and pastel blue. Swirl the icing on top of the cakes, then sprinkle over the silver balls.

Whether it's 4th July, Bonfire Night or Bastille Day, these sparkling celebration cakes are just the thing to serve when the night sky is exploding with brightly coloured stars. Take a plate of these dense, moist, citrusy chocolate cakes topped with mini-sparklers outside while you watch the fireworks.

FIREWORK CUPCAKES

115 g plain flour

3 tablespoons cocoa powder

½ teaspoon bicarbonate of soda

50 g caster sugar

120 ml freshly squeezed orange juice

grated zest of 1 unwaxed orange

3 tablespoons sunflower oil

1½ teaspoons white wine vinegar

to decorate

100 g dark chocolate, finely chopped

100 ml double cream

edible silver balls or stars

12 mini-sparklers

a 12-hole cupcake tin, lined with paper cases

makes 12

Preheat the oven to 180°C (350°F) Gas 4.

Combine the flour, cocoa powder, bicarbonate of soda and sugar in a bowl. Sift into a larger bowl and make a well in the centre.

Combine the orange juice and zest, oil and vinegar in a jug and pour into the dry ingredients. Quickly stir together until combined, then spoon the mixture into the paper cases. (It should be quite liquid and gooey, so you may find a small ladle useful.)

Bake in the preheated oven for about 15 minutes until risen and firm on top and a skewer inserted in the centre comes out clean. Transfer to a wire rack to cool.

To decorate, put the chocolate in a heatproof bowl. Heat the cream in a saucepan until almost boiling, then pour over the chocolate. Leave to melt for about 5 minutes, then stir until smooth and creamy. Leave to cool for 5–10 minutes more until thick and glossy, then spread over the cakes.

Sprinkle the frosted cakes with tiny silver balls or stars and stick a sparkler in the centre of each one. Light the sparklers before serving.

INDULGENT CUPCAKES

The idea of these cupcakes is for the cake to rise over the height of the paper case so you can slice it off and then sandwich it with cream and strawberries – so avoid very deep paper cases for this recipe. Go for pretty ones, about 2.5 cm deep instead, and serve them up at an afternoon tea party.

VICTORIA CUPCAKES

115 g unsalted butter, at room temperature

115 g caster sugar

2 eggs

115 g self-raising flour

½ teaspoon baking powder

1 teaspoon vanilla extract

to decorate

2 tablespoons strawberry jam

180 ml double cream

225 g strawberries, thickly sliced

icing sugar, for dusting

a 12-hole cupcake tin, lined with paper cases

makes 12

Preheat the oven to 180°C (350°F) Gas 4.

Beat the butter and sugar together until pale and fluffy, then beat in the eggs, one at a time. Combine the flour and baking powder and sift into the mixture. Fold in, then stir in the vanilla extract.

Spoon the mixture into the paper cases and bake in the preheated oven for about 17 minutes until risen and golden and a skewer inserted in the centre comes out clean. Transfer to a wire rack to cool.

To decorate, using a serrated knife, carefully slice the top off each cake, down to the level of the paper case. Spread each cake with about ½ teaspoon jam.

Whip the cream and spoon on top of the jam-covered cakes, then top with slices of strawberries. Replace the top of each cake and dust with icing sugar.

The combination of chocolate, marshmallows and nuts in these sweet and sticky cakes is a taste of pure indulgence. If you've got a really sweet tooth, sprinkle a few extra mini-marshmallows on top along with the nuts and chocolate chips, or if you prefer a more adult version, leave them spread simply with the chocolate topping.

ROCKY ROAD CUPCAKES

115 g unsalted butter, at room temperature

100 g caster sugar

2 eggs

115 g self-raising flour

3 tablespoons cocoa powder

3 tablespoons milk

25 g white chocolate chips

50 g mini-marshmallows

25 g flaked almonds or slivered brazil nuts

to decorate

100 g dark chocolate, finely chopped

100 ml double cream

25 g flaked almonds or slivered brazil nuts

25 g white chocolate chips

mini-marshmallows (optional)

a 12-hole cupcake tin, lined with paper cases

makes 12

Preheat the oven to 180°C (350°F) Gas 4.

Beat the butter and sugar together in a bowl until pale and fluffy, then beat in the eggs, one at a time. Sift the flour and cocoa powder into the mixture and fold in. Stir in the milk, followed by the chocolate chips, marshmallows and nuts.

Spoon the mixture into the paper cases and bake in the preheated oven for about 18 minutes until risen and the tops spring back when lightly pressed. Transfer to a wire rack to cool.

To decorate, put the chocolate in a heatproof bowl. Heat the cream in a saucepan until almost boiling, then pour over the chocolate and leave to melt for about 5 minutes. Stir until smooth and creamy, then leave to cool for about 30 minutes until thick and glossy.

Spread the chocolate mixture over the cakes and sprinkle with the nuts, chocolate chips and marshmallows, if using.

Sinking your teeth into these golden, buttery cakes with their gooey lemon centre and sticky white Italian meringue frosting is a sheer taste of heaven. Try to find a really good-quality lemon curd for the filling to give these little cakes their really intense, lemony flavour. One simply won't be enough!

LEMON MERINGUE CUPCAKES

115 g unsalted butter, at room temperature

100 g caster sugar

2 eggs

115 g self-raising flour

grated zest and freshly squeezed juice of 1 unwaxed lemon

3 tablespoons good-quality lemon curd

to decorate

150 g caster sugar

2 egg whites

a 12-hole cupcake tin, lined with paper cases

a piping bag, fitted with a star-shaped nozzle (optional)

makes 12

Preheat the oven to 180°C (350°F) Gas 4.

Beat the butter and sugar together in a bowl until pale and fluffy, then beat in the eggs, one at a time. Sift the flour into the mixture and fold in, then stir in the lemon zest and juice.

Spoon a good dollop of the mixture into each paper case and make an indentation in the centre with the back of a teaspoon. Drop in a dollop of lemon curd, then top with the remaining cake mixture. Bake in the preheated oven for about 17 minutes until risen and golden. Transfer to a wire rack to cool.

To decorate, put the sugar and egg whites in a bowl and set over a saucepan of simmering water. Whisk constantly for about 5 minutes until the mixture is thick and glossy and stands in peaks. Use the piping bag fitted with a star-shaped nozzle to pipe a whirl onto the top of each cake or swirl the meringue over the cakes using a spoon. The frosting will firm up as the cakes sit, so for a soft meringue, leave to set for at least 30 minutes, and for a firm one, leave to set for at least 3 hours.

For trifle-lovers everywhere, these are the ultimate indulgence – moist, crumbly sponge with chunks of raspberries and a drizzle of kirsch, then smothered in creamy custard and topped with more fruit. You can use any seasonal berries you like here. Pick the most perfect, luscious fruits you can find to decorate the cakes.

RASPBERRY TRIFLE CUPCAKES

115 g unsalted butter, at room temperature

115 g caster sugar

2 eggs

115 g self-raising flour

140 g raspberries, halved

to decorate

1 tablespoon kirsch

60 ml double cream

125 ml fresh custard

200 g raspberries and redcurrants, or other seasonal berries of your choice

a 12-hole cupcake tin, lined with paper cases

makes 12

Preheat the oven to 180°C (350°F) Gas 4.

Beat the butter and sugar together in a bowl until pale and fluffy, then beat in the eggs, one at a time. Sift the flour into the mixture and fold in, then fold in the raspberries.

Spoon the mixture into the paper cases and bake in the preheated oven for 18 minutes until risen and golden and a skewer inserted in the centre comes out clean. Transfer to a wire rack to cool.

To decorate, prick each cupcake all over with a skewer and pour ¼ teaspoon kirsch over each one, allowing it to soak into the cake. Whip the cream, then fold in the custard and spoon on top of the cakes. Top each cake with raspberries and redcurrants, or seasonal berries of your choice.

With a gooey chocolate and hazelnut centre, these luscious cakes are deliciously tender. Stirring chocolate and hazelnut spread into the frosting gives it a wonderfully nutty taste to complement the toasted hazelnuts on top. Serve them up as a rich treat alongside a good cup of mid-morning coffee.

GOOEY CHOCOLATE AND HAZELNUT CUPCAKES

75 g dark chocolate, chopped

100 g unsalted butter, at room temperature

100 g caster sugar

2 eggs

25 g blanched hazelnuts, ground

100 g self-raising flour

100 g chocolate and hazelnut spread, such as Nutella

to decorate

100 g dark chocolate, finely chopped

100 ml double cream

2 tablespoons chocolate and hazelnut spread, such as Nutella

about 25 g blanched hazelnuts, toasted and cut into large pieces

a 12-hole cupcake tin, lined with paper cases

makes 12

Preheat the oven to 180°C (350°F) Gas 4.

Put the chocolate in a heatproof bowl set over a pan of gently simmering water. Do not let the bowl touch the water. Leave until almost melted. Remove from the heat and leave to cool.

Beat the butter and sugar together in a bowl until pale and fluffy, then beat in the eggs, one at a time. Stir in the hazelnuts, then sift the flour into the mixture and fold in. Stir in the melted chocolate.

Drop ½ heaped tablespoonful of the mixture into each paper case, then flatten and make an indentation in the centre using the back of a teaspoon. Drop a generous dollop of chocolate spread into the centre of each one, then top with the remaining cake mixture. Bake in the preheated oven for about 18 minutes until risen and the tops spring back when gently pressed. Transfer to a wire rack to cool.

To decorate, put the chocolate in a heatproof bowl. Heat the cream in a saucepan until almost boiling, then pour over the chocolate and leave to stand for about 5 minutes. Stir until smooth and creamy, then leave to cool for about 30 minutes until thick and glossy.

Spread the frosting over the cakes and arrange a cluster of nuts in the centre of each one.

Golden vanilla sponge topped with a thick layer of creamy vanilla and white chocolate cheesecake and decorated with fresh strawberries is the ultimate treat. These cupcakes are best chilled so that the creamy topping sets but if you just can't wait, they're equally good while it's still soft.

VANILLA AND WHITE CHOCOLATE CHEESECAKE CUPCAKES

115 g unsalted butter, at room temperature

115 g caster sugar

2 eggs

115 g self-raising flour

½ teaspoon vanilla extract

2 tablespoons milk

to decorate

175 g white chocolate, chopped

175 g cream cheese

6 tablespoons crème fraîche

1½ teaspoons vanilla extract

6 tablespoons icing sugar, sifted

fresh strawberries

a 12-hole cupcake tin, lined with paper cases

makes 12

Preheat the oven to 180°C (350°F) Gas 4.

Beat the butter and sugar together in a bowl until pale and fluffy, then beat in the eggs, one at a time. Sift the flour into the mixture and fold in, then stir in the vanilla extract and milk.

Spoon the mixture into the paper cases. Bake in the preheated oven for about 10 minutes until risen and golden and a skewer inserted in the centre comes out clean. Transfer to a wire rack to cool.

To decorate, check that none of the cakes have risen above the rim of the paper cases. If any have, carefully slice off the top using a serrated knife to create a flat surface.

Put the chocolate in a heatproof bowl set over a pan of gently simmering water. Do not let the bowl touch the water. Leave until almost melted, then set aside to cool slightly. Beat the cream cheese, crème fraîche, vanilla extract and sugar together in a separate bowl, then beat in the melted chocolate.

Smooth the cream cheese mixture over the cakes, up to the rim of the paper cases, then refrigerate for at least 1½ hours until set. Decorate with fresh strawberries and serve.

For anyone who loves florentines, these inspired cupcakes offer the perfect combination, but in a cuter, more colourful package. A rich, white chocolate crumb is finished with chewy glacé fruits, nuts and a sticky white chocolate topping. Offer them to a friend who needs cheering up and watch their face light up!

FLORENTINE CUPCAKES

60 g white chocolate, chopped

115 g unsalted butter, at room temperature

115 g caster sugar

2 eggs

115 g self-raising flour

½ teaspoon vanilla extract

to decorate

85 g white chocolate, chopped

4 tablespoons double cream

50 g glacé fruits, such as citrus peel, apricots, pineapple and angelica, chopped

6 glacé cherries, chopped

50 g shelled nuts, such as walnuts, pistachios and hazelnuts, chopped

25 g flaked almonds (optional)

two 12-hole mini-cupcake tins or a baking sheet, plus 24 petits fours cases

makes 24

Preheat the oven to 180°C (350°F) Gas 4, then line the mini-cupcake tin with petit fours cases. (If you don't have a mini-cupcake tin, arrange the cases on a baking sheet; the cases should be able to cope with such a small amount of mixture.)

Put the chocolate in a heatproof bowl set over a pan of gently simmering water. Do not let the bowl touch the water. Leave until almost melted, then set aside to cool slightly.

Beat together the butter and sugar in a bowl until pale and fluffy, then beat in the eggs, one at a time. Sift the flour into the mixture and fold in, then stir in the vanilla extract and melted chocolate.

Spoon the mixture into the petits fours cases and bake in the preheated oven for about 18 minutes until golden and a skewer inserted in the centre comes out clean. Transfer to a wire rack to cool.

To decorate, put the chocolate and cream in a heatproof bowl set over a pan of gently simmering water. Do not let the bowl touch the water. Leave until the chocolate is just starting to melt, then remove from the heat and stir until smooth. Stir in the glacé fruits and the nuts, then refrigerate for 20 minutes before spooning on top of the cakes. Decorate with flaked almonds, if using.

These cupcakes, made using a classic Genoese sponge, are light and creamy and perfect for serving in summer when fresh soft berries are sweet, juicy and in season. Experiment with any ripe berries you can find. Because the sponge contains no fat, the cakes don't keep well, so they are best eaten on the day they're made.

FRESH FRUIT CUPCAKES

2 eggs

60 g caster sugar

1 teaspoon vanilla extract

90 g plain flour

to decorate

180 ml double cream

250 g fresh summer berries, such as strawberries, blueberries, raspberries and redcurrants

icing sugar, for dusting

a 12-hole cupcake tin, lined with paper cases

makes 12

Preheat the oven to 180°C (350°F) Gas 4.

Put the eggs and sugar in a large bowl and whisk for about 10 minutes until thick and pale. Add the vanilla extract. Sift the flour into a separate bowl twice, then sift into the egg mixture and fold in.

Spoon the mixture into the paper cases and bake in the preheated oven for about 12 minutes until risen and golden and a skewer inserted in the centre comes out clean. Transfer to a wire rack to cool.

To decorate, whip the cream in a bowl until it stands in peaks, then swirl over the cakes. Top with fresh berries, dust with icing sugar and serve immediately.

These rich, dark, chocolatey cakes studded with chocolate-covered coffee beans and topped with a creamy coffee-butter frosting are simply divine. Dusted with grated chocolate, they look like a plateful of mini cappuccinos – but don't eat too many or they might keep you awake all night!

CHOCA-MOCHA CUPCAKES

100 g dark chocolate, chopped

150 g unsalted butter,
at room temperature

150 g caster sugar

2 eggs

2 tablespoons cocoa powder

100 g self-raising flour

2 teaspoons instant coffee,
dissolved in 1 tablespoon
boiling water

40 g chocolate-covered
coffee beans

to decorate

100 g unsalted butter,
at room temperature

200 g icing sugar, sifted

2 teaspoons instant coffee,
dissolved in 1 tablespoon
boiling water

dark chocolate, grated

*a 12-hole cupcake tin,
lined with paper cases*

makes 12

Preheat the oven to 180°C (350°F) Gas 4.

Put the chocolate in a heatproof bowl set over a pan of gently simmering water. Do not let the bowl touch the water. Leave until almost melted, then set aside to cool slightly.

Beat the butter and sugar together in a bowl until pale and fluffy, then beat in the eggs, one at a time. Stir in the melted chocolate and cocoa powder. Sift the flour into the mixture and stir in, then stir in the coffee, followed by the coffee beans.

Spoon the mixture into the paper cases and bake in the preheated oven for about 20 minutes until risen and a skewer inserted in the centre comes out clean. Transfer to a wire rack to cool.

To decorate, beat the butter, sugar and coffee together in a bowl until pale and fluffy. Spread the mixture smoothly over the cakes and sprinkle with grated chocolate.

When you're desperate for a week on a desert island but haven't got the time or money, try one of these cupcakes instead. They may not be quite the same as a tropical holiday, but the dense little pineapple cakes smothered in rich, creamy coconut frosting and topped with sweet, juicy wedges of mango come in a fabulous second best!

TROPICAL CUPCAKES

85 g unsalted butter, at room temperature

100 g light brown sugar

2 eggs

4 tablespoons crème fraîche

115 g self-raising flour

¼ teaspoon mixed spice

a 227-g tin pineapple rings, drained and diced (140 g drained weight)

to decorate

140 g mascarpone

2 tablespoons creamed coconut

40 g icing sugar, sifted

1 mango, stoned, peeled and cut into wedges

a 12-hole cupcake tin, lined with paper cases

makes 12

Preheat the oven to 180°C (350°F) Gas 4.

Beat the butter and sugar together in a bowl until pale and fluffy, then beat in the eggs, one at a time. Stir in the crème fraîche, then sift the flour and mixed spice over the top and fold in. Add the pineapple and fold in.

Spoon the mixture into the paper cases and bake in the preheated oven for about 20 minutes until risen and golden and a skewer inserted in the centre comes out clean. Transfer to a wire rack to cool.

To decorate, put the mascarpone, creamed coconut and sugar in a bowl and beat together until smooth and creamy. Swirl the frosting on top of the cakes and decorate with wedges of mango.

Topped with a cool, creamy mascarpone topping and golden shards of praline, these little cakes offer a pure taste of heaven. A hint of bitter coffee brings out and enhances the flavour of the nutty praline. If you're a real coffee fiend, try one of these cupcakes with a cup of strong, black coffee.

COFFEE AND PRALINE CUPCAKES

115 g caster sugar

60 g blanched hazelnuts

115 g unsalted butter, at room temperature

2 eggs

80 g self-raising flour

1 teaspoon baking powder

2 teaspoons instant coffee, dissolved in 1 tablespoon boiling water

to decorate

60 g caster sugar

40 g blanched hazelnuts, roughly chopped

100 g mascarpone

115 g icing sugar, sifted

1 teaspoon instant coffee, dissolved in ½ tablespoon boiling water

a 12-hole cupcake tin, lined with paper cases

makes 12

Preheat the oven to 180°C (350°F) Gas 4. Line a baking sheet with greaseproof paper.

Put half the sugar in a saucepan and heat gently, stirring, for about 5 minutes until melted and pale gold. Add the hazelnuts and cook, stirring, for about 1 minute, then pour onto the lined baking sheet and leave to harden for at least 20 minutes.

Break the hardened praline into pieces and place in a food processor, then process until finely ground. Set aside.

Beat the butter and the remaining sugar together in a bowl until pale and fluffy, then beat in the ground praline. Beat in the eggs, one at a time, then sift the flour and baking powder into the mixture and fold in. Stir in the coffee.

Spoon the mixture into the paper cases and bake in the preheated oven for about 16 minutes until risen and golden and a skewer inserted in the centre comes out clean. Transfer to a wire rack to cool.

To decorate, put the caster sugar in a saucepan and heat gently, stirring, for about 5 minutes until melted and pale gold. Add the hazelnuts and cook, stirring, for about 30 seconds, then pour onto the lined baking sheet. Leave to harden for about 20 minutes, then break into small shards.

Beat the mascarpone and icing sugar together in a bowl until smooth and creamy, then stir in the coffee. Swirl the mixture onto the cakes and decorate with shards of praline.

Inspired by the classic Black Forest gateau, these dinky, crumbly chocolate cakes are studded with sweet, sticky cherries and spiked with kirsch. If you really want to go overboard on indulgence, serve them topped with a dollop of whipped cream as well, and shave over some dark chocolate curls.

BLACK FOREST CUPCAKES

90 g dark chocolate, chopped

115 g unsalted butter, at room temperature

115 g caster sugar

2 eggs

2 tablespoons ground almonds

150 g self-raising flour

1 tablespoon cocoa powder

2 tablespoons kirsch

50 g glacé cherries, halved

to decorate

100 g dark chocolate, finely chopped, plus extra to decorate

100 ml double cream

1 tablespoon kirsch

12 glacé cherries

a 12-hole cupcake tin, lined with paper cases

makes 12

Preheat the oven to 180°C (350°F) Gas 4.

Put the chocolate in a heatproof bowl set over a pan of gently simmering water. Do not let the bowl touch the water. Leave until almost melted, then set aside to cool slightly.

Beat the butter and sugar together in a bowl until pale and fluffy, then beat in the eggs, one at a time. Beat in the melted chocolate, then stir in the almonds. Sift the flour and cocoa powder into the mixture and fold in, followed by the kirsch and the glacé cherries.

Spoon the mixture into the paper cases and bake in the preheated oven for about 20 minutes until a skewer inserted in the centre comes out clean. Transfer to a wire rack to cool.

To decorate, put the chocolate in a heatproof bowl. Heat the cream in a saucepan until almost boiling, then pour over the chocolate and leave to melt for about 5 minutes. Stir until smooth and creamy, then stir in the kirsch and leave to cool for about 1 hour until thick and glossy. Spread the frosting over the cakes and top with a glacé cherry. Using a vegetable peeler, make some chocolate shavings with the extra dark chocolate and pop them on top of the cakes.

Topped with a rich, gooey, sticky frosting, these wickedly dense, chocolatey cupcakes studded with chunks of sweet, peppery stem ginger are the only cupcake choice for ginger-loving chocaholics. Expecting friends round for tea? Surprise them by whipping up a batch of these irresistible little treats.

CHOCOLATE AND GINGER CUPCAKES

80 g dark chocolate, chopped

100 g unsalted butter, at room temperature

100 g caster sugar

2 eggs

115 g self-raising flour

2 tablespoons cocoa powder

3 balls of stem ginger in syrup, drained and chopped

to decorate

100 g dark chocolate, finely chopped

50 g white marshmallows, snipped into pieces

100 ml double cream

a 12-hole cupcake tin, lined with paper cases

makes 12

Preheat the oven to 180°C (350°F) Gas 4.

Put the chocolate in a heatproof bowl set over a pan of gently simmering water. Do not let the bowl touch the water. Leave until almost melted, then set aside to cool for about 5 minutes.

Beat the butter and sugar together until pale and fluffy, then beat in the eggs, one at a time. Stir in the melted chocolate, then sift the flour and cocoa powder into the mixture and fold in. Add the ginger and stir in.

Spoon the mixture into the paper cases and bake in the preheated oven for about 18 minutes until a skewer inserted in the centre comes out clean. Transfer to a wire rack to cool.

To decorate, put half the chocolate and the marshmallows in a heatproof bowl and set over a pan of barely simmering water. Heat gently, stirring occasionally, until the chocolate and marshmallows are almost melted. Remove the bowl from the heat and continue stirring until the marshmallows are completely melted.

Add the remaining chocolate and stir until melted, then stir in the cream. Leave to cool for about 2 hours until thick, then swirl on top of the cakes.

Inspired by the classic banoffee pie, these creamy cakes are simply to die for. The tender, moist banana cakes are packed with nuggets of chewy toffee, then topped with whipped cream, sweet and sticky dulce de leche and fresh banana. If you can't find it, you can make your own dulce de leche by following the instructions below.

BANOFFEE CUPCAKES

60 g unsalted butter, at room temperature

70 g soft brown sugar

1 egg, beaten

1 ripe banana, mashed

115 g self-raising flour

50 g chewy toffees, chopped

to decorate

180 ml double cream, whipped

3–4 tablespoons dulce de leche

1 banana, sliced

a 12-hole cupcake tin, lined with just 10 paper cases

makes 10

Preheat the oven to 180°C (350°F) Gas 4.

Beat the butter and sugar together in a bowl until creamy, then beat in the egg, a little at a time. Fold in the mashed banana, then sift the flour into the mixture and fold in, followed by the toffees.

Spoon the mixture into the paper cases and bake in the preheated oven for about 16 minutes until risen and a skewer inserted in the centre comes out clean. Transfer to a wire rack to cool.

To decorate, swirl the cream over each of the cakes, then drizzle with a spoonful of dulce de leche and top with slices of banana.

Note: Dulce de leche is a sweet, gooey toffee sauce from Argentina and it is available from larger supermarkets. If you can't find it, you can make it yourself. Put a sealed tin of condensed milk in a saucepan, pour over boiling water to cover and boil for 3 hours, adding more water as necessary so that the tin is always covered. Remove from the pan and leave to cool completely before opening using a tin opener. Stir well to make a smooth sauce before spooning over the cakes.

CUPCAKES
FOR SPECIAL DIETS

Perfect for anyone on a dairy-free diet, these tender cupcakes are delicately scented with fragrant cardamom and pistachio and drenched in a tangy, intensely flavoured sticky lime syrup. The courgette may sound like an odd ingredient but it gives the cupcakes a wonderfully moist texture.

COURGETTE, PISTACHIO AND LIME CUPCAKES

seeds from 3 cardamom pods, crushed

1 egg

60 ml sunflower oil

100 g caster sugar

100 g courgette, grated

50 g shelled pistachio nuts, chopped

115 g self-raising flour

½ teaspoon baking powder

to decorate

finely grated zest and freshly squeezed juice of 2 unwaxed limes

85 g caster sugar

40 g shelled pistachio nuts, chopped

a 12-hole cupcake tin, lined with paper cases

makes 12

Preheat the oven to 160°C (325°F) Gas 3.

Put the crushed cardamom seeds in a bowl with the egg, oil and sugar, then beat until smooth and creamy. Add the courgette and nuts and stir together until well mixed. Combine the flour and baking powder, then sift into the courgette mixture and fold in.

Spoon the mixture into the paper cases and bake in the preheated oven for 18–20 minutes until risen and golden and a skewer inserted in the centre comes out clean. Transfer to a wire rack to cool.

To decorate, put the lime zest and juice, and the sugar into a saucepan. Heat gently, stirring, until the sugar has dissolved, then bring to the boil. Boil for about 1 minute, then remove from the heat. Stir in the nuts and leave to cool slightly until the syrup starts to thicken, then spoon over the cakes.

Naturally gluten-free, these light chocolate cakes made with potato flour and spread with a rich chocolate cream cheese frosting are great for anyone following a gluten- or nut-free diet. Top them with grated chocolate for a sophisticated treat, or sprinkle with edible sparkles for something more playful.

CHOCOLATE CREAM CHEESE CUPCAKES

40 g unsalted butter, melted

1 tablespoon cocoa powder

115 g caster sugar

25 g cream cheese

1 egg

½ teaspoon vanilla extract

60 g potato flour

½ teaspoon baking powder

¼ teaspoon bicarbonate of soda

1 tablespoon milk

to decorate

25 g dark chocolate, plus extra to decorate

150 g cream cheese

50 g icing sugar, sifted

¼ teaspoon vanilla extract

a 12-hole cupcake tin, lined with paper cases

makes 12

Preheat the oven to 180°C (350°C) Gas 4.

In a bowl, stir together the butter and cocoa powder, then stir in the sugar. Add the cream cheese and beat in. Beat in the egg, then stir in the vanilla extract. Add the flour, baking powder and bicarbonate of soda and stir together. Stir in the milk.

Spoon the mixture into the paper cases and bake in the preheated oven for about 16 minutes until risen and a skewer inserted in the centre comes out clean. Transfer to a wire rack to cool.

To decorate, put the chocolate in a heatproof bowl set over a pan of gently simmering water. Do not let the bowl touch the water. Leave until almost melted. Remove from the heat and leave to cool for about 10 minutes.

Beat together the melted chocolate, cream cheese, sugar and vanilla extract until creamy, then spread the frosting on top of the cakes. Using a vegetable peeler, make chocolate shavings and scatter on top of the cakes.

Almost like mini-Dundee cakes, these rich cupcakes flavoured with brandy are a great gluten-free choice when you need a mid-afternoon treat with a cup of tea. At Christmas-time, you could leave off the almonds and decorate with marzipan, royal icing and a sprig of holly or a festive snowman if you like.

RICH FRUIT CUPCAKES

60 g unsalted butter, at room temperature

40 g soft light brown sugar

1 egg, beaten

60 g rice flour

1 teaspoon baking powder

2 tablespoons ground almonds

1 tablespoon brandy

115 g luxury mixed dried fruit

40 g blanched almonds

a 12-hole cupcake tin, lined with paper cases

makes 12

Preheat the oven to 160°C (325°F) Gas 3.

Beat together the butter and sugar in a bowl until smooth and creamy, then gradually beat in the egg. Combine the flour and baking powder, then sift into the mixture. Stir in, followed by the ground almonds, brandy and dried fruit.

Spoon the mixture into the paper cases and top each cake with three or four blanched almonds. Bake in the preheated oven for 25 minutes until a skewer inserted in the centre comes out clean. Transfer to a wire rack to cool.

Moist and chewy with a subtly spiced crumb and a simple orange icing, these cupcakes are best eaten on the day you make them. With their seasonal pumpkin filling and orange appearance, they would be perfect served at a Halloween party or as a healthier alternative to the usual 'trick or treat' candies.

LOW-FAT PUMPKIN AND RICOTTA CUPCAKES

115 g pumpkin or butternut squash flesh, diced

150 g plain flour

1½ teaspoons baking powder

60 g caster sugar

¼ teaspoon ground cinnamon

1 egg

2 tablespoons sunflower oil

125 ml semi-skimmed milk

½ teaspoon vanilla extract

60 g ricotta

to decorate

2 tablespoons freshly squeezed orange juice

200 g icing sugar, sifted

grated unwaxed orange zest

a 12-hole cupcake tin, lined with paper cases

makes 12

Preheat the oven to 200°C (400°C) Gas 6.

Put the pumpkin on a square of aluminium foil and fold up the edges to seal. Bake in the preheated oven for about 20 minutes until tender. Tip out into a bowl and mash roughly with a fork.

Reduce the oven temperature to 180°C (350°F) Gas 4.

Combine the flour, baking powder, sugar and cinnamon and sift together into a bowl. In a separate bowl, combine the egg, oil, milk, vanilla extract and ricotta and whisk together until smooth. Stir in the mashed pumpkin. Pour into the dry ingredients and fold together until just combined.

Spoon the mixture into the paper cases and bake in the preheated oven for about 25 minutes until risen and a skewer inserted in the centre comes out clean. Transfer to a wire rack and leave to cool.

To decorate, put the orange juice in a bowl, then sift the sugar into the bowl and stir until smooth. Spoon on top of the cakes and sprinkle with grated orange zest.

Bake up a batch of these cupcakes for vegan friends, or anyone following a nut-, egg- or dairy-free diet. The dark, bitter-chocolate cakes with a hint of coffee are a delicious combination of soft, squidgy crumb and sweet, fudgy frosting. They're so moreish that everyone will love them, whatever their diet!

DARK CHOCOLATE CUPCAKES

115 g plain flour

½ teaspoon bicarbonate of soda

3 tablespoons cocoa powder

115 g caster sugar

3 tablespoons sunflower oil

1 teaspoon instant coffee, dissolved in 2 teaspoons boiling water

1½ teaspoons white wine vinegar

to decorate

2 tablespoons sunflower oil

1½ tablespoons cocoa powder

1 teaspoon instant coffee, dissolved in 2 tablespoons boiling water

150 g icing sugar, sifted

a 12-hole cupcake tin, lined with paper cases

makes 12

Preheat the oven to 180°C (350°F) Gas 4.

Combine the flour, bicarbonate of soda, cocoa powder and sugar and sift together into a bowl. Make a well in the centre. Pour in 125 ml water, the oil, coffee and vinegar and stir together.

Spoon the mixture into the paper cases and bake in the preheated oven for about 15 minutes until risen and firm and a skewer inserted in the centre comes out clean. Transfer to a wire rack to cool.

To decorate, put the oil, cocoa powder and coffee in a heatproof bowl set over a pan of gently simmering water and stir. Do not let the bowl touch the water. Gradually pour in the sugar and stir for about 2 minutes until thick and glossy. Add about ½ teaspoon more water to thin slightly and stir for another minute, then spoon the frosting over the cakes.

Warm, nutty and fragrant with orange zest, these light, fluffy, gluten- and dairy-free cakes are plain and simple without being in the least bit dull. They melt in the mouth and are perfect served still warm from the oven. For those who can't do without a little indulgence, serve them with a dollop of crème fraîche on top.

ORANGE AND ALMOND CUPCAKES

2 eggs

90 g caster sugar

grated zest of 1 unwaxed orange

80 g ground almonds

3 tablespoons potato flour

about 40 g flaked almonds

icing sugar, for dusting

a 12-hole cupcake tin, lined with paper cases

makes 12

Preheat the oven to 170°C (325°F) Gas 3.

Put the eggs and sugar in a bowl and whisk for 5–10 minutes until thick and pale. Add the orange zest, then sift the ground almonds and potato flour into the mixture and fold in.

Spoon the mixture into the paper cases and sprinkle the flaked almonds over the top. Bake in the preheated oven for about 22 minutes until risen and golden and a skewer inserted in the centre comes out clean. Transfer to a wire rack and leave to cool slightly before dusting with icing sugar and serving.

These soft, chewy, egg-free cupcakes topped with a sweet and zesty cream cheese frosting are based on a classic muffin mixture and best eaten on the day you make them. Kids love them, so they're a great choice if you know a child with an egg allergy. Just remember to check they're not allergic to nuts.

BANANA, HONEY AND PECAN CUPCAKES

150 g self-raising flour

½ teaspoon baking powder

50 g shelled pecan nuts, chopped

2 ripe bananas

3 tablespoons sunflower oil

4 tablespoons honey

60 ml milk

to decorate

150 g cream cheese

50 g icing sugar, sifted

1 teaspoon freshly squeezed lime juice

slivered pecans, to decorate

a 12-hole cupcake tin, lined with paper cases

makes 12

Preheat the oven to 180°C (350°C) Gas 4.

Combine the flour and baking powder and sift into a bowl. Add the nuts and stir together. Make a well in the centre.

In a separate bowl, mash the bananas with a fork. Add the oil, honey and milk and stir together. Tip the mixture into the dry ingredients and stir together until just combined. (Don't overmix.)

Spoon the mixture into the paper cases and bake in the preheated oven for 20 minutes until risen and golden and skewer inserted in the centre comes out clean. Transfer to a wire rack to cool.

To decorate, beat together the cream cheese, sugar and lime juice until smooth and creamy, then swirl on top of the cakes. Decorate with slivered pecans.

With half the fat of a classic cupcake, these tempting little devils offer you a cupcake treat but with half the guilt attached. The prune and Armagnac purée stirred into the cakes gives them a distinctive flavour and lovely moist texture. They're ideal for those with a sweet tooth who also like a little alcoholic kick in their desserts.

PRUNE AND ARMAGNAC CUPCAKES

60 g ready-to-eat dried prunes

3 tablespoons boiling water

1 tablespoon Armagnac

60 g unsalted butter,
at room temperature

60 g light brown sugar

1 egg, beaten

115 g self-raising flour

½ teaspoon baking powder

to decorate

200 g icing sugar, sifted

2 tablespoons freshly squeezed
lemon juice

12 ready-to-eat dried prunes

*a 12-hole cupcake tin,
lined with paper cases*

makes 12

Preheat the oven to 180°C (350°F) Gas 4.

Put the prunes and boiling water in a blender and blend to make a purée. (Don't worry if it's not entirely smooth.) Set aside to cool, then stir in the Armagnac.

Beat together the butter and sugar, then stir in the prune purée. Beat in the egg, a little at a time, then sift the flour and baking powder into the mixture and fold in.

Spoon the mixture into the paper cases and bake in the preheated oven for about 18 minutes until golden and a skewer inserted in the centre comes out clean. Transfer to a wire rack to cool.

To decorate, stir together the sugar and lemon juice until smooth, then spoon on top of the cakes. Top each one with a prune.

Not so much cupcakes as cup-meringues, these pretty little confections are nut- and gluten-free as well as being low in fat. And the dark chocolate drizzled on top is suitable for people on a dairy-free diet too. So whether you're on a diet or suffering from food allergies, these are cupcakes that everyone can enjoy.

MERINGUE SPRINKLE CUPCAKES

2 egg whites

100 g caster sugar

to decorate

30 g dark chocolate, chopped

hundreds and thousands

a 12-hole cupcake tin, lined with paper cases

makes 12

Preheat the oven to 150°C (300°F) Gas 2.

Put the egg whites in a spotlessly clean bowl and whisk until they stand in peaks. Sprinkle over a tablespoonful of sugar and whisk in. Continue whisking in the sugar a tablespoonful at a time until the egg whites are thick and glossy.

Using two tablespoons, shape the meringue into balls and drop into the paper cases. Bake in the preheated oven for 10 minutes, then reduce the temperature to 140°C (275°F) Gas 1 and bake for a further 40 minutes. Turn off the oven but leave the meringues in the oven to cool.

To decorate, put the chocolate in a heatproof bowl set over a pan of gently simmering water. Do not let the bowl touch the water. Leave until melted, then drizzle over the meringues and sprinkle with hundreds and thousands.

These little cupcakes are considerably lower in fat than a classic coffee and walnut cake and yet they taste just as delicious. They are made with a butter-free whisked sponge and the ricotta frosting contains about one-eighth of the fat of a classic buttercream. Super easy to throw together, they are the perfect choice for afternoon tea.

COFFEE AND WALNUT CUPCAKES

2 eggs

60 g caster sugar

1 teaspoon instant coffee, dissolved in 1 teaspoon boiling water

85 g plain flour

to decorate

85 g ricotta

25 g icing sugar, sifted

½ teaspoon instant coffee, dissolved in ½ teaspoon boiling water

12 walnut halves

a 12-hole cupcake tin, lined with paper cases

makes 12

Preheat the oven to 180°C (350°F) Gas 4.

Put the eggs and sugar in a bowl and whisk for about 10 minutes until pale and thick. Drizzle the coffee into the mixture and fold in using a large metal spoon. Sift the flour into a separate bowl, then sift into the mixture and fold in.

Spoon the mixture into the paper cases and bake in the preheated oven for 12 minutes until risen and golden and a skewer inserted in the centre comes out clean. Transfer to a wire rack to cool.

To decorate, beat together the ricotta, sugar and coffee until smooth and creamy, then spoon on top of the cakes and top each one with a walnut half.

KIDS' CUPCAKES

You can't get much cuter than a plateful of these pink piggies sitting on the tea table. Except perhaps a gang of mini-farmers in checked shirts and matching dungarees! So why not go with the animal theme and throw a farmyard tea party? Decorating these cupcakes is a little fiddly, but the final result is well worth the effort!

PINK PIGGY CUPCAKES

115 g unsalted butter, at room temperature

115 g caster sugar

2 eggs

115 g self-raising flour

1 teaspoon vanilla extract

2 tablespoons milk

to decorate

pink food colouring

400 g ready-to-roll fondant icing

2 tablespoons raspberry jam, sieved

dark purple or black food paste colouring

a 12-hole cupcake tin, lined with paper cases

three cookie cutters, one about the same size as your cupcake cases, one slightly smaller, and one very small

makes 12

Preheat the oven to 180°C (350°F) Gas 4.

Beat the butter and sugar together until pale and fluffy, then beat in the eggs, one at a time. Sift the flour into the mixture and fold in, then stir in the vanilla extract and milk.

Spoon the mixture into the paper cases and bake in the preheated oven for about 17 minutes until risen and golden and a skewer inserted into the centre comes out clean. Transfer to a wire rack to cool.

To decorate, add a couple of drops of pink food colouring to the fondant icing and knead until well blended to make a pale pink icing. Roll out the icing between two sheets of greaseproof paper or clingfilm to about 3 mm thick. Stamp out 12 rounds using the largest cookie cutter. Using a pastry brush, brush the tops of the cakes with jam and gently press the pink rounds on top.

Using the scraps, roll out 12 rounds with the medium-sized cookie cutter, brush one side with water and stick onto the cupcakes. Then with the smallest cutter, stamp out 12 rounds of icing and brush one side with water. Place in the centre of each cake to make a nose and press gently in place. Using a round skewer, make two round holes next to each other for nostrils.

Using the remaining scraps of icing, cut out 24 small oval shapes for ears then brush the back of each lightly with water and fix two in place on top of each piggy's head, turning the tips of the ears up slightly. Roll a little icing into corkscrew tails and stick on.

Dip the flat end of a wooden skewer in the purple or black colouring paste. Dab two eyes above the nose, then draw a little mouth under the nose. Voilà!

Children will love learning to count with these fun number cakes with a sweet fruity crumb. You need to make the number decorations the day before to give them time to harden, so allow plenty of time to prepare ahead. This recipe suggests using three colours for the icing and numbers but you can use as many as you like.

NUMBER CUPCAKES

115 g unsalted butter, at room temperature

115 g caster sugar

2 eggs

115 g self-raising flour

115 g dried fruit

to decorate

50 g ready-to-roll fondant icing

yellow food colouring

green food colouring

150 g mascarpone

50 g icing sugar, sifted

1 teaspoon freshly squeezed lemon juice

blue food colouring

a 12-hole cupcake tin, lined with paper cases

mini-number cookie cutters

makes 12

First make the number decorations. Divide the fondant icing into two pieces. Add a couple of drops of yellow food colouring to one piece and green to the other and knead until the colours are well blended. Roll out each piece between two sheets of greaseproof paper or clingfilm to about 3 mm thick. Stamp out as many numbers as you like using the cookie cutters. Leave to dry overnight until hard.

Preheat the oven to 180°C (350°F) Gas 4.

Beat the butter and sugar together until pale and fluffy, then beat in the eggs, one at a time. Sift the flour into the mixture and fold in, then stir in the dried fruit.

Spoon the mixture into the paper cases and bake in the preheated oven for 17 minutes until risen and golden and a skewer inserted in the centre comes out clean. Transfer to a wire rack to cool.

To decorate, put the mascarpone, sugar and lemon juice in a bowl and beat together until smooth and creamy. Add a few drops of blue food colouring and stir in until evenly mixed. Spread the icing on top of the cakes and stick the numbers into the icing so they stand up slightly.

These pretty spotty cupcakes look incredibly professional but are so easy to make. You can use plain round cookie cutters, or crinkle-cut ones which will give a pretty flowery effect. And of course, it's up to you which colours you use – you can easily adapt the recipe to match a party theme or colour scheme.

SPOTTY CUPCAKES

115 g unsalted butter, at room temperature

115 g caster sugar

2 eggs

115 g self-raising flour

1 teaspoon vanilla extract

2 tablespoons milk

to decorate

450 g ready-to-roll fondant icing

pink food colouring

green food colouring

2 tablespoons apricot jam, sieved

a 12-hole cupcake tin, lined with paper cases

a cookie cutter, 6.5 cm in diameter

a cookie cutter, 2 cm in diameter

makes 12

Preheat the oven to 180°C (350°F) Gas 4.

Beat the butter and sugar together in a bowl until pale and fluffy, then beat in the eggs, one at a time. Sift the flour into the mixture and fold in, then stir in the vanilla extract and milk.

Spoon the mixture into the paper cases and bake in the preheated oven for about 17 minutes until risen and golden and a skewer inserted in the centre comes out clean. Transfer to a wire rack to cool.

To decorate, divide the fondant icing into two pieces. Add a couple of drops of pink food colouring to one piece and green to the other and knead until the colours are well blended. Roll out each piece between two sheets of greaseproof paper or clingfilm to about 4 mm thick, and large enough so that you will be able to cut out six rounds from each piece using the 6.5-cm cookie cutter.

Using the 2-cm cookie cutter, cut rounds from the two sheets of icing – spacing them about 1 cm apart – to create a spotty pattern. Very carefully, without tearing the icing, remove the pink rounds and swap them with the green rounds so you end up with two pink and green spotty sheets of icing. Gently go over the icing with the rolling pin until it's about 3 mm thick.

Using the 6.5-cm cookie cutter, stamp out six rounds from each sheet. Brush the top of each cake with apricot jam, then gently lay a round on top and pat in place.

These decorate-your-own-cakes are always a hit at kids' parties. And they're just as good served up at the end of a grown-up dinner party instead of dessert! Everyone will love getting creative and trying to produce the most outlandish cupcake at the table. Just be sure to make plenty of icing and search out lots of pretty decorations.

DO-IT-YOURSELF PARTY CAKES

115 g unsalted butter, at room temperature

115 g caster sugar

2 eggs

115 g self-raising flour

1½ tablespoons cocoa powder

to decorate

175 g unsalted butter, at room temperature

450 g icing sugar, sifted

2 tablespoons milk

lilac, yellow and green food colouring

brightly coloured candies, such as dolly mixture, Smarties and Jelly Tots

coloured sprinkles such as hundreds and thousands, sugar flowers and edible coloured balls

a 12-hole cupcake tin, lined with paper cases

makes 12

Preheat the oven to 180°C (350°F) Gas 4.

Beat the butter and sugar in a bowl until pale and fluffy, then beat in the eggs, one at a time. Sift the flour and cocoa powder into the mixture and fold in.

Spoon the mixture into the paper cases and bake in the preheated oven for about 17 minutes until risen and a skewer inserted in the centre comes out clean. Transfer to a wire rack to cool completely.

To decorate, beat the butter until soft, then add the sugar and milk and beat until smooth and creamy. Divide the icing among three bowls. Add a few drops of food colouring to each one and stir well to make a vibrant lilac, yellow and green. Spoon into serving bowls.

Arrange the cakes on a plate and put the decorations in individual bowls alongside the bowls of icing. Let the kids or guests decorate their own cakes.

Children love these little chocolate nests with pretty pastel-coloured eggs nestling inside. They're easy to make and kids will have a great time helping to decorate them – perfect if you're looking for a fun activity on a rainy afternoon. They are also a good choice for a sweet treat at Easter time.

BIRD'S NEST CUPCAKES

115 g unsalted butter, at room temperature

115 g caster sugar

2 eggs

115 g self-raising flour

1½ tablespoons cocoa powder

2 tablespoons milk

to decorate

150 g mascarpone

50 g icing sugar, sifted

1 tablespoon cocoa powder

2–3 chocolate flake bars

36 sugar-coated chocolate eggs (about 100 g)

a 12-hole cupcake tin, lined with paper cases

makes 12

Preheat the oven to 180°C (350°F) Gas 4.

Beat the butter and sugar together in a bowl until pale and fluffy, then beat in the eggs, one at a time. Sift the flour and cocoa powder into the mixture and fold in, then stir in the milk.

Spoon the mixture into the paper cases and bake in the preheated oven for 18 minutes until risen and a skewer inserted in the centre comes out clean. Transfer to a wire rack to cool.

To decorate, put the mascarpone, sugar and cocoa powder in a bowl and beat together until smooth and creamy. Pop a dollop of frosting on top of each cake.

Break the chocolate flake bars into shards resembling twigs, then arrange them on top of the frosting to create 12 little bird's nests. Finish off with three eggs in the centre of each nest.

These are an all-time favourite – just as good for a teatime snack as they are on a party table. They're blissfully easy to make and kids will have great fun helping to choose sweets for the topping. Hundreds and thousands are the classic decoration but you can buy all kinds of tiny, coloured shapes that will work just as well.

VANILLA BUTTERCREAM CUPCAKES

115 g unsalted butter, at room temperature

115 g caster sugar

2 eggs

115 g self-raising flour

1 teaspoon vanilla extract

2 tablespoons milk

to decorate

85 g unsalted butter, at room temperature

225 g icing sugar, sifted

1 tablespoon milk

¼ teaspoon vanilla extract

yellow food colouring

coloured sugar sprinkles

a 12-hole cupcake tin, lined with paper cases

makes 12

Preheat the oven to 180°C (350°F) Gas 4.

Beat the butter and sugar together in a bowl until pale and fluffy, then beat in the eggs, one at a time. Sift the flour into the mixture and fold in, then stir in the vanilla extract and milk.

Spoon the mixture into the paper cases and bake in the preheated oven for about 18 minutes until risen and golden and a skewer inserted in the centre comes out clean. Transfer to a wire rack to cool.

To decorate the cakes, put the butter in a bowl and beat until smooth and creamy. Add the sugar, milk and vanilla extract and beat together until smooth and creamy. Add a few drops of the food colouring and stir until well mixed and you have achieved the desired colour.

Swirl the icing on top of the cupcakes, then sprinkle over the coloured sprinkles.

These pretty little cakes offer a surprise when you bite into them – they're a beautiful pale pink inside! The white chocolate frosting needs to thicken for a couple of hours before you can decorate the cakes, so be sure to allow plenty of time before serving. Add fewer candies for a more elegant look.

CANDY CUPCAKES

115 g unsalted butter, at room temperature

115 g caster sugar

2 eggs

115 g self-raising flour

pink food colouring

to decorate

100 g white chocolate, finely chopped

80 ml double cream

dolly mixture or coloured candies, to decorate

a 12-hole cupcake tin, lined with paper cases

makes 12

Preheat the oven to 180°C (350°F) Gas 4.

Beat the butter and sugar together in a bowl until pale and fluffy, then beat in the eggs, one at a time. Sift the flour into the mixture and fold in. Add a dash of pink food colouring and stir in until well mixed and the cake mixture is an even pale pink.

Spoon the mixture into the paper cases and bake in the preheated oven for about 17 minutes until risen and golden and a skewer inserted into the centre comes out clean. Transfer to a wire rack to cool.

To decorate, put the chocolate in a heatproof bowl. Heat the cream until almost boiling, then pour over the chopped chocolate and leave to stand for about 5 minutes. Stir until melted and smooth. Refrigerate for about 2 hours until thick and glossy then spread over the cakes. Decorate with dolly mixture or coloured candies.

These cute cupcakes topped with a smooth, creamy, not-too-sweet mascarpone frosting look like little hedgehogs. Get the kids to help out decorating the cakes – they'll just love sticking the chocolate chips into the creamy frosting. They make a nice change from chocolate chip cookies as a little treat after school.

CHOCOLATE CHIP CUPCAKES

115 g unsalted butter, at room temperature

115 g caster sugar

2 eggs

115 g self-raising flour

1 teaspoon vanilla extract

100 g dark chocolate chips

to decorate

150 g mascarpone

50 g icing sugar, sifted

¼ teaspoon vanilla extract

25 g dark chocolate chips, chilled

a 12-hole cupcake tin, lined with paper cases

makes 12

Preheat the oven to 180°C (350°F) Gas 4.

Beat the butter and sugar together in a bowl until pale and fluffy, then beat in the eggs, one at a time. Sift the flour into the mixture and fold in, then stir in the vanilla extract. Sprinkle over the chocolate chips and fold in.

Spoon the mixture into the paper cases and bake in the preheated oven for about 17 minutes until risen and golden and a skewer inserted in the centre comes out clean. Transfer to a wire rack to cool.

To decorate, put the mascarpone, sugar and vanilla extract in a bowl and beat together until smooth and creamy. Spread the frosting on the cakes, then carefully press the chocolate chips on top of the cakes like little hedgehog spines. (Handle the chocolate chips as little as possible to avoid them melting.)

Just like a batch of sugary little treasure chests, these pretty bejewelled cupcakes will appeal to girly girls – but cheeky little pirates won't be able to keep their hands off them either! Make sure you break the boiled sweets into small enough pieces so that they aren't a choking hazard for small children.

HIDDEN TREASURE CUPCAKES

115 g unsalted butter, at room temperature

115 g caster sugar

2 eggs

115 g self-raising flour

grated zest of 1 unwaxed orange

3 tablespoons candied peel (optional)

to decorate

125 g fruity boiled sweets

100 g icing sugar, sifted

1 tablespoon freshly squeezed lemon juice

orange food colouring

a 12-hole cupcake tin, lined with paper cases

makes 12

Preheat the oven to 180°C (350°F) Gas 4.

Beat the butter and sugar together in a bowl until pale and fluffy, then beat in the eggs, one at a time. Sift the flour into the mixture and fold in, then stir in the orange zest and candied peel, if using.

Spoon the mixture into the paper cases and bake in the preheated oven for 17 minutes until golden and a skewer inserted in the centre comes out clean. Transfer to a wire rack to cool.

To decorate, leaving the sweets in their wrappers, hit them with a rolling pin to break into large pieces. (Don't smash them into dust!) Tip the broken sweets into a bowl and set aside.

Stir together the sugar and lemon juice and add a couple of drops of the food colouring to make an orange icing. Spoon the icing onto the cakes and pile the broken sweet 'jewels' on top.

These cupcakes are perfect for serving as dessert for a party – but they can be messy so be sure to have plenty of napkins at the ready for wiping sticky fingers! I like vanilla ice cream with mine, but you can choose any flavour you like – chocolate, strawberry and mint-choc-chip are always favourites.

ICE CREAM CUPCAKES

60 g unsalted butter, at room temperature

60 g caster sugar

1 egg, beaten

60 g self-raising flour

to decorate

60 g dark chocolate, chopped

2½ tablespoons double cream

1 tablespoon golden syrup

ice cream

a 12-hole cupcake tin, lined with paper cases

makes 12

Preheat the oven to 180°C (350°F) Gas 4.

Beat the butter and sugar in a bowl until pale and fluffy, then gradually beat in the egg. Sift the flour into the mixture and fold in.

Spoon the mixture into the paper cases and bake in the preheated oven for about 15 minutes until risen and golden and a skewer inserted in the centre comes out clean. Transfer to a wire rack and leave to cool completely. When they've cooled, use a serrated knife to carefully cut a shallow hole out of the centre of the cupcakes. Keep what you've cut out for lids.

To decorate, put the chocolate, cream and syrup in a small saucepan and warm gently, stirring, until the chocolate starts to melt. Remove the pan from the heat and continue stirring until smooth and creamy and the chocolate has completely melted.

Using a melon baller, make small scoops of ice cream and place on top of the cupcakes. Replace the lids of the cakes, then spoon over the chocolate sauce and serve immediately.

These pretty pink cupcakes with a rippled, jammy crumb are always a hit with kids. If your kids want to decorate the cakes themselves, you might want to leave off the piped spirals – but they'll look just as lovely simply topped with raspberries. They're also gorgeous for adults to give to a loved one as a token of their affection.

RASPBERRY RIPPLE CUPCAKES

115 g unsalted butter, at room temperature

115 g caster sugar

2 eggs

115 g self-raising flour

2 tablespoons raspberry jam

to decorate

150 g icing sugar, sifted

1–1½ tablespoons freshly squeezed lemon juice

pink food colouring

12 raspberries

a 12-hole cupcake tin, lined with paper cases

a piping bag, fitted with a narrow nozzle

makes 12

Preheat the oven to 180°C (350°F) Gas 4.

Beat the butter and sugar together in a bowl until pale and fluffy, then beat in the eggs, one at a time. Sift the flour into the mixture and fold in.

Put the jam in a small bowl and stir well until runny. Spoon dollops of the cake mixture into the paper cases and flatten slightly with the back of a teaspoon, making a slight indent in the centre. Drop about ¼ teaspoon jam in the centre of each indent. Top with the remaining cake mixture and drizzle about ¼ teaspoon more jam on top of each one. Draw a skewer through each cake about three times to ripple the mixture. Bake in the preheated oven for about 18 minutes until risen and golden. Transfer to a wire rack to cool.

To decorate, put the sugar in a bowl and gradually stir in the lemon juice until you have a thick, spooning consistency. Reserve a couple of tablespoonfuls of the icing, then add one or two drops of pink food colouring to the remaining icing. Stir well until you have the desired colour.

Spoon the icing onto the cakes. Spoon the reserved white icing into the piping bag fitted with a narrow nozzle. Pipe a white spiral onto each cake, then put a raspberry in the centre of each one.

These adorable cakes are perfect served with a big glass of milk at teatime. For a party, why not cover the table with a green cloth and simply scatter the cakes around among the other plates of goodies – like flowers growing in a meadow. They're so pretty nobody will be able to resist stealing one or two!

FLOWER CUPCAKES

115 g unsalted butter,
at room temperature

115 g caster sugar

2 eggs

115 g self-raising flour

grated zest of 1 unwaxed lemon

to decorate

150 g icing sugar, sifted

1–1½ tablespoons freshly
squeezed lemon juice

pink and green food colouring
(or any colours of your choice)

sugar rosettes

*a 12-hole cupcake tin,
lined with paper cases*

makes 12

Preheat the oven to 180°C (350°F) Gas 4.

Beat the butter and sugar together in a bowl until pale and fluffy, then beat in the eggs, one at a time. Sift the flour into the mixture and fold in, then stir in the lemon zest.

Spoon the mixture into the paper cases and bake in the preheated oven for about 18 minutes until risen and golden and a skewer inserted in the centre comes out clean. Transfer to a wire rack to cool.

To decorate, put the sugar and lemon juice in a bowl and stir together until smooth and creamy. It should be thick and spoonable, but not too runny. Divide the icing among two bowls, add a few drops of food colouring to each one and stir well to make a good vibrant pink and green.

Spoon the icing onto the cakes, allowing it to spread slightly so that it resembles flower petals, then drop a sugar rosette into the centre of each flower.

These little cakes are great for kids' parties. You can use them as place names at the tea table, or let everyone find their own special cake on the plate when it comes to dessert. Alternatively, they make a great going-home gift, with each child taking home their own personalized cake in a party bag.

SPECIAL NAME CUPCAKES

60 g unsalted butter, at room temperature

60 g caster sugar

1 egg, beaten

60 g self-raising flour

½ teaspoon grated unwaxed orange zest

to decorate

coloured card, pens, glitter and glue or double-sided tape

12 cocktail sticks

60 g unsalted butter, at room temperature

150 g icing sugar, sifted

½–1 tablespoon milk

½ teaspoon grated unwaxed orange zest

orange food colouring

a 12-hole cupcake tin, lined with paper cases

a piping bag, fitted with a star-shaped nozzle

makes 12

Preheat the oven to 180°C (350°F) Gas 4.

Beat the butter and sugar together in a bowl until pale and fluffy, then gradually beat in the egg. Sift the flour into the mixture and fold in, then stir in the orange zest.

Spoon the mixture into the paper cases and bake in the preheated oven for 15 minutes until risen and golden and a skewer inserted in the centre comes out clean. Transfer to a wire rack to cool.

To decorate, cut out about twenty-four 8 x 3-cm rectangles from the coloured card and fold in half. Hold the cocktail sticks inside the folded card and glue the two pieces of card together to make a flag. Snip the flags to turn them into any shape you like. Write names on the flags and decorate with pens and glitter.

Put the butter, sugar, milk and orange zest in a bowl and beat together until smooth and creamy. Add a few drops of orange food colouring and stir in. Spoon the icing into the piping bag fitted with a star-shaped nozzle and pipe the icing on top of the cakes. Stick one or two flags into each cake.

suppliers and stockists

Cakes Cookies & Crafts Shop
www.cakescookiesandcraftsshop.co.uk
Tel: 01524 389 684
Online suppliers of every kind of baking equipment you might ever need: lots and lots of paper cupcake cases, tins, silicone moulds, cookie cutters, edible decorations and plenty more.

David Mellor
www.davidmellordesign.com
4 Sloane Square
London SW1W 8EE
Tel: 020 7730 4259
Well-stocked kitchen shop and online store.

Divertimenti
www.divertimenti.co.uk
227–229 Brompton Road
London SW3 2EP
Tel: 020 7581 8065
33–34 Marylebone High Street
London W1U 4PT
Tel: 020 7935 0689
Divertimenti shops in South Kensington and the West End stock an enormous range of cooking utensils, pots and pans, copper, earthenware, hand-decorated tableware, cutlery and glassware – just about everything a food lover could possibly want. They also have a well-regarded cookery and wine school. Their online shop is equally comprehensive, with individual, reusable silicone muffin and cupcake cases.

Jane Asher
www.janeasher.com
22–24 Cale Street
London SW3 3QU
Tel: 020 7584 6177
Britain's foremost cake and sugarcraft supplier, for all your decorating needs!

John Lewis
www.johnlewis.com
A lovely range of bakeware, from vintage-style mixing bowls and measuring cups to ceramic cupcake cups, heart-shaped and silicone cupcake tins.

Lakeland
www.lakeland.co.uk
Huge selection of kitchen and baking equipment, such as cupcake tins, cake decorations, storage containers, etc., as well as a stand designed especially to display cupcakes.

The Pod Company
www.thepodcompany.co.uk
Unique and unusual gift ideas, including stylish kitchenware.

Something
www.something-shop.com
58 Lamb's Conduit Street
Bloomsbury
London WC1N 3LW
Tel: 020 7430 1516
Gorgeous gift shop selling all sorts of desirable items, such as glass cake stands and vintage tea plates.

Squires Shop
www.squires-shop.com
Tel: 0845 2255671
Online specialist suppliers of all things to do with cakes, including decorating, food colouring and sugarcraft. Even has a section on classic sweets!

index